LET'S TALK

MUTUAL FUNDS

LET'S TALK MUTUAL FUNDS

A SYSTEMATIC, SMART WAY TO MAKE THEM WORK FOR YOU

Monika Halan

HARPER BUSINESS
An Imprint of HarperCollins Publishers

First published in India by Harper Business
An imprint of HarperCollins *Publishers* 2023
4th Floor, Tower A, Building No. 10, Phase II,
DLF Cyber City, Gurugram, Haryana – 122002
www.harpercollins.co.in

7

P-ISBN: 978-93-5699-146-0
E-ISBN: 978-93-5699-135-4

Typeset in 13/17 Requiem at
Manipal Technologies, Manipal

Printed and bound at
Repro India Limited

MIX
Paper | Supporting responsible forestry
FSC® C047271

This book is produced from independently certified FSC® paper
to ensure responsible forest management.

HarperCollins PublishersMacken House, 39/40 Mayor Street Upper, Dublin 1,
D01 C9W8, Ireland

CONTENTS

1

MONEY IS GOOD

Money is good. Everyone should have enough and more. It is how you earn it and where you choose to spend it that matters.

Most people don't begin thinking about money till they need to. Usually when you begin supporting lifestyle costs as a young adult and your parents appear to be putting obstacles in your way, you realize that dad as the ATM might have a use-by date. Or when you finally step out on your own to live in another city on a small first salary, you suddenly discover the merits of home cooking—something that your mom had been raging about forever. Your money now ends before your month. Each month. Every time. You remember money when you need it suddenly in an emergency if you lose your job or need to pay a medical bill. Or when you want to buy a house and your money just does not stretch to the equated monthly instalment (EMI) needed. Then, when you are nearing retirement and you realize that your money is simply not going to stretch as far as you had imagined it would. The rose-tinted images of retirement don't show the full picture—they omit the stash of purchasing power needed for that future to manifest.

Most people don't think about money unless they have to, because in most homes, talking about money is strictly taboo. 'Why bother, main hoon na—I'm there' is the most-heard middle-class Indian dad statement. After the sex conversation, it is the money talk that is the most difficult in families. But, there is a reason why money conversations are taboo and some of that has to do with India's past.

Once the foreign invasions began, the historically wealthy nation began to slowly move towards poverty. It took centuries for the vibrant trade and commerce that used to be centred around temples as banks and hubs to wither away. The last push towards moving poverty from a temporary place to believing it is permanent was given by the British over their years of subjugation of India. The final kick was the Bengal famine of 1943. Imagine the plight of a nation's psyche that saw around three million people starving to death. When a nation does not even have food, it does believe that poverty is their fate and nothing will improve their lot. If you know you can't have something, it is better to discard it. Notice how it is called haath ka mael or dirt of the hand in Hindi, or how the rich are called filthy. The idea that someone can get rich without doing something wrong is still new to India, steeped as it is in the socialist past of the post-Independence years.

Nothing mirrors the attitudes towards wealth as well as Hindi cinema. *Mother India* in 1957 had the evil moneylender preying upon the poor and using his power to crush them. All that the poor have is their morality that they refuse to give up on. The 1970s saw the shift in the evil rich to the smuggler. In the epic film *Deewar*, the rich guy had his gaadi, bangla and daulat—but the poor guy had his mum, but no car, bungalow or wealth. The movie checks every box on how poverty is a badge of honour and the rich are corrupt. By the time the decade was getting over, India, under the rule of Indira Gandhi, turned further left, ideologically. Our very Preamble to the Constitution was changed in 1976 to include the words secular and socialist. Over the past decades, the leaders of post-Independence India had decided that profit was a bad word and business owners were evil. This was the time of nationalization of banks, insurance firms, coal mines, airlines, and of throwing out multinationals such as Coca-Cola.

The epic film *Kaala Patthar* documents that attitude, where the evil guy was the coal mine owner feeding off the blood, sweat and life of the poor coal miners and their families. The evil guy is rich, the good guys are poor. Their salvation lies in the hands of the government through nationalization.

Then India got a little bit of economic freedom—more than four decades after political freedom—when in 1991, gates to privatization and reducing the stranglehold of bureaucrats on the economic lifeblood was loosened. It took another decade for the message to get to Mumbai, but the movie *Dil Chahta Hai* at the turn of the millennium nailed the change in the attitude towards wealth of a growing slice of the Indian population. The movie took wealth for granted as a backdrop and even had a woman drinking wine without being either a prostitute or a bad girl! And then, in 2019, *Gully Boy* has a Mumbai shanty boy dreaming of making it big—not for his dying mum or his marriageable-age sister, but for himself. Apna time aayega—my time will come—he says as a mantra over and over again.

Money has slowly moved from something evil to something aspirational, but our basic attitude towards it has not changed. I was to give a talk at a school known for being the cradle of the children of Mumbai's richie-rich families. What will I tell the sons and daughters of top industrialists, movie stars, bankers, lawyers about money was my mental hurdle.

When I spoke to the two students of class eleven who were organizing the event, I discussed the topic that I like to speak to young adults in the twenty-first century about—why you should be rich. I said that money is good—it is not evil. It is how we earn it and how we spend it that might have moral values, but by itself the desire to be affluent is good.

They were silent for almost thirty seconds. One of them asked if I could tell their parents that it was okay to aspire for money. That was surprising. I had thought that a general conversation at their homes would be around wealth. So, I dug deeper and found that the outright desire to make money is still not a topic accepted at the dinner table even in the wealthiest of homes in the presence of school-going children. The discomfort around money, wealth and its consumption is still very strong.

Not only are discussions around money frowned upon at home, the education system does not empower and equip the next generations to manage their finances. Colleges of engineering, medicine, astrophysics, law and economics might put young adults through rigorous coursework and exams, but the graduates are clueless about what to do with their first salary they worked so desperately hard to get.

While the market underneath has changed, Indians remain overinvested in fixed deposits (FDs), gold, life insurance and real estate and fear newer products like mutual funds that have been designed for an average retail investor. The same investor seeking a guarantee from an FD or a money-back insurance policy might periodically pump money into the latest Ponzi scheme wildly, just like so many people did during the 2020–21 crypto 'currency' episode.

But let me ask you this: hum hain naye, andaaz kyun ho puraanaa—if we are new, then why should our style be so fuddy-duddy? Why should investors not take sensible risks using products specially designed and regulated for them?

There are five things that need to be changed in the way middle-class India thinks about its money.

One, stop thinking about money as a one-time decision. It is a recurring decision throughout your life. The earlier you have a first-principles–based mental roadmap, the better your money will serve you. I have seen people consider every investment decision in isolation.

That there is a larger money story that should define your investing lifetime is fully lost to them. Each decision actually depends on other choices made and cannot be made without looking at the larger financial picture of the family. Where to put Rs 5 lakh today or which five funds to buy is the way they approach their investing decisions. This usually ends badly because unless there is a thought-through strategy, you will bounce from last year's winner to this year's loser. The day you really get the fact that there is no escape from dealing with your money-life is when your control over your finances begins.

Two, investing long term is not your first goal at all. The goal is to have a financial plan that covers all the contours of an average money-life, such as having liquidity when you need it, having money when you want to buy a house, having buffer cash for when things go wrong. The larger plan includes a cash-flow system, an emergency fund and building life and medical insurances before we begin investing. If you have not, then it is a good idea to read my book *Let's Talk Money* (2018) that explains this in detail. We need at least thirteen-fourteen products in our portfolio, therefore we need a product category that can offer the most options. Mutual funds allow us to target our immediate and short-, medium- and long-term goals, giving us that one product category that can solve most financial problems.

Three, you just have to stop killing your money in toxic insurance-plus-investment plans. These plans give neither a good life cover nor good returns. Worse, they are built like traps and you stand to lose a chunk of your money if you don't stay with the policy for the fifteen–twenty years that it is sold for. Go back and reread the life insurance chapter in *Let's Talk Money* if your blood has unfrozen from the shock of first reading that chapter.

Four, rethink the idea that real estate is your best long-term investment. This is an illiquid asset—you can't sell a loo when you need some money, you need to sell the whole three BHK. There are large transaction costs to buying and selling and worse, cash deals are still common in real estate. Also, the appreciation of this asset that is taken for granted is simply not true. As I write this in 2023, the nuclear winter of real estate is already a decade old and there is no way of knowing how much air is still there in the prices. According to the yield metric (annual rent divided by market price of the property), there is still enough room for prices to fall as the yields today are still just 1.5–2 per cent. These need to be at least 4 per cent for the property to be fairly priced even for living in it. For an investment built on a loan, the yield needs to be higher.

Five, you have no option but to give your money an equity exposure, or an allocation to stocks. Equity allocation must not be misunderstood to mean only buying shares yourself or trading them through the day. This means using mutual funds to invest into the Indian stock market for a lower risk way to create wealth. You have to stop thinking of the stock market as if it is a gambling den. It can be for people who like to punt. But it is also a place for taking structured risk with products, such as index funds (explained on page 72, Chapter 4), that help you build a corpus at a very low cost.

This is a book about mutual funds—a great product for retail investors in India. I say this because the rules for this part of the capital markets are the tightest. This book is a sequel to *Let's Talk Money* and I am writing it on popular demand! Many of you reached back after reading the first book to say that I got you all ready to invest but you needed to know more about mutual funds. So here it is. I do hope this opens up a new way of being in control of your money and your life.

Let's mutual fund!

2

MUTUAL FUND BASICS

Money is your one true friend till your last breath. After that it does not matter. But till then, look after it.

What is a mutual fund?

Essentially, a mutual fund is just a pipe that connects your savings to a bunch of securities such as stocks and bonds. Let's stay with stocks first and imagine each stock to be like a bead in a box. There are thousands of beads in the market. You can buy a few beads from the entire box. Some of these beads will turn out to be precious and will double or triple your money. Some will be semiprecious stones that will give a good profit. Some will be just wood or stone and will actually be worth less than what you paid for a bead. Others will turn to sand in some time and your money will be lost. You want to make your savings work harder and want to buy some beads so that your get a good return. How will you choose five beads out of the multitude on offer? Can you examine each bead? Do you have the time, the jauhari (discerning) eye to evaluate the intrinsic value of the beads? Each of them looks shiny and bright. How will you choose? Suppose you do the needed homework and choose five beads and spend Rs 1 lakh, but a year later all of them turn out to be sand. Your Rs 1 lakh falls to nothing—you lose all your money. What if all of them turn out to be precious and your money doubles? What if two are precious and three are sand? What if pure luck gets all five beads to be precious? It will be bad luck to get all five made of sand. But you won't know till a year later what you had bought, so how do you take a decision now?

What if you could hire an expert to do the bead picking? You pay for his services, including costs of buying and selling to maintain your bead portfolio. But such an expert will charge a lot and you might not be able to afford such a person. Good fund managers might cost more than what you earn in a year, let along what you want to invest! But what if investors like you got together, pooled your savings and hired an expert in beads? This expert will have some rules of the game that she must follow and collectively you will oversee that she remains true to the game. You will evaluate her on the performance year after year and if you find that she does not do her job well and another group of investors have a better bead picker, you will fire her and rehire that somebody else who is better. The per person cost of the expert will be small compared to one person hiring the expert for individual bead picking.

Then, because some bead pickers ran off with investors' money, the government put in place some rules. Now there is a way for you to buy beads collectively with other people using a regulated way that has an oversight of rules and regulation of a marketplace, that would not only reduce your costs, but also provide safety against fraud and somebody vanishing with your money. The judgement of the expert may also not be 100 per cent right, but because he has a large amount of money, he is able to diversify, or expand his bead selection to at least thirty–fifty beads, up from the five you could afford. Even if some beads turn to sand, the overall loss will get diluted. So also the overall profit will get diluted as some beads will do well and others won't. Your risk goes down and you will hold a varied set of beads that should give you an overall good profit.

This is a very simplistic way of looking at how the mutual fund industry and markets work—just replace beads with stocks and bonds and you begin to get a mind-picture of what the whole story is about. A mutual fund is simply an investment vehicle that you use to buy stocks, bonds, gold, real estate and combinations of these. A mutual fund scheme collects money from investors offering to invest it in a certain way. It could just be an equity scheme that wants to invest the money in large-caps. (Flip ahead to page 49, Chapter 4 to understand market caps.) Or in mid-caps. Or in pharma stocks. Or in foreign stocks. Or ask you for a wall-to-wall mandate to do whatever the fund manager wants with the aim of generating a good return. It could just be bonds that mature in about three months, giving you a very short-term product. Or bonds that mature in a year, giving you a slightly longer investing horizon.

If you first understand the purpose of a mutual fund, it is much easier to comprehend the way the market is set up. It helps you stay wary of fundamentally flawed arguments such as 'SIPs give better interest'. Mutual funds are market-linked products and do not give a guaranteed return or interest and SIP is not a product, but a route, as we will find out later. The purpose of savings is to convert them into investments. This is done through products such as bank FDs, PPF, stocks, bonds, real estate and gold that belong to different asset classes—equity, debt and real assets.

Equity means stocks of both listed and unlisted companies. Debt spans the entire range of fixed-return products like FDs, PPF, government bonds and riskier products like corporate deposits and corporate bonds. You have the option to invest directly in stocks, bonds and gold, and many people do that with good results. But others find it useful to go through an entity called a mutual fund that makes investing in the underlying (equity, debt and gold) less risky.

A mutual fund collects money from investors and deploys it in a bunch of listed securities. These securities are 'listed' or available for trade on a stock market. (I encourage you to read the basics of the market in *Let's Talk Money* before you read on, in case you are not following this.) Essentially, what a mutual fund does is to form a link between investors and stocks, bonds and gold bought with the aim of increasing the value of the money invested. By how much the value will increase will depend on what category of mutual fund the investor chooses. (Turn to page 45, Chapter 4 to understand categories better.) An investor seeks expert fund management and greater safety of diversification since each scheme holds between twenty-five and fifty stocks or bonds or both, rather than spend time trying to do this on his own.

Mutual funds because investing is more than just high returns

Most first-time investors into mutual funds get attracted by the stories of high returns. It is true that post-tax returns on mutual funds can be better than the more traditional options, but most investors make the error of comparing apples with oranges. It would be incorrect to compare an FD return with an all equity fund. But even if we compare apples with apples and see that within the same asset class of debt (FD, bonds and so on), a portfolio of bonds through a mutual fund has the potential to give higher returns than FDs or any money-back life insurance policy. We will understand the returns piece better in Chapter 6 starting page 111. And then the post-tax return story will unfold from page 162 in Chapter 8.

Higher returns is just one of the attributes of a mutual fund that investors most obviously see. But there is much more to investing than just returns. Liquidity, for example, is a very important attribute. To be of use, the money has to be available. Let's understand liquidity by comparing a mutual fund to a real estate investment. You know how tough it is to sell a property, how long it takes and how you need to sell the full property even though you may only need a part of the money just then. Mutual funds provide this easy liquidity since your money returns to you between one and four working days. You need not sell your entire holding and can either target the money or some of the units you own. When we look at an investment as more than just returns, we begin to see why mutual funds are so important in our financial lives. Well-chosen mutual funds allow us to target future liquidity needs while earning higher returns than what a safer FD route would get.

A friend had bought some land just outside the small-town Indian city he lives in twenty years ago. Of course, in twenty years, the lakhs became crores. His small-scale business took a hit and he needed to sell the land to repay all the debts he and his family had accumulated. The land sale would have more than paid the debt and would have left something for his savings as well. But for two years, he could not get a buyer at the price he wanted. Deals would come near and then collapse. Then there was the issue of buyers wanting to pay between 40 per cent to 60 per cent in cash (non-tax paid 'black' money). He had bank loans he had to repay and needed 'white' money. So he had to find out how to turn black to white—it costs between 5 per cent and 15 per cent, he told me. Then the local mafia got to know of this large land deal in their area and he began to get calls for their cut. One deal went through but the person backed out and to get his advance money back, threatened to put the land into dispute so that the case would drag for decades. The friend finally found an all-white deal buyer and got out of the financial mess, but the journey was harrowing.

When you compare this story of delay, tension, threats and fear to simply redeeming your mutual fund portfolio by tapping a few keys on your laptop, you begin to understand that an investment is not just about a high return, it is also about what it costs to buy, sell and hold and how easy it is to buy and sell that asset.

Another factor that appeals to me about mutual funds is the sheer ease of transaction, once you have jumped through the hoop of doing the paperwork and onboarded the platform through which you will transact. Once you understand that investments are not a once-a-year sprint but a regular month-on-month outflow into a carefully chosen bunch of products, then ease of transaction becomes supremely important. The once-a-year approach usually works with an agent coming home and getting you to write a cheque. A monthly approach means that you need to set up the system. I find investing in mutual funds easy to do with lots of options on how to set it up. (Flip over to page 248 in Chapter 13 to see the various options to buy mutual funds.) You can either choose to work through somebody who takes a cheque every time to invest or you can set up a system through your bank, or through your demat account, or you can use some of the many fintech applications, or you can go direct through Mutual Fund Utility, the transaction platform developed by the mutual fund industry. Whatever your route, once you set it up with links to your Invest-It account, or the bank account in which you hold your savings ready for investments, investing is a few key-strokes away. I like that transactions cost me very little time and money. The time investment is front loaded to set up your investing system through the platform you decide to use. Then it is just using it over the rest of your life. Build the pipelines once and then use them forever.

A third reason that makes mutual funds attractive is the ease of comparison for investors. It is important that the financial product can be compared across its competitors on various metrics of performance, costs and risk. The market regulator—the Securities and Exchange Board of India (SEBI)—has standardized the product features and disclosures to such an extent that it is now easy to compare funds across their category competitors, against a benchmark to see how well the product does. In comparison, when you are sold a traditional insurance policy, there is just a lot of fuzzy information given to you. You are told that there is a good return, that there is a bonus, that there is a death benefit and there is a free life cover. But if you want to compare these features across various similar policies, it is very difficult to do. The agents will mostly tell you that it cannot be done. But move to mutual funds and you realize that every small detail like risk metrics, costs and performance history can be compared. Independent data analytic firms such as Value Research, Credit Rating Information Services of India Limited (CRISIL) and Morningstar allow you to look at their data and use tools online to compare on metrics including expense ratio, risk and returns over time. They also give benchmark comparisons so that you can easily see if the scheme that you want to invest in has been performing well or not and whether the managed fund is worth the cost you are paying or not.

And then there is the issue of cost. Costs to enter, maintain and exit a product are important in a financial product specially if it is to be held for a long period of time. Again, take real estate for example—it is both an expensive asset in terms of time and money to buy and sell. Brokerage is usually 1 per cent of the deal and then there is stamp duty to be paid when you buy and capital gains tax when you sell. While holding the property, tax and the cost of renovation and maintenance are to be paid every year. There is a capital cost each time one tenant leaves ahead of the next one coming on board when you refurbish the property. There can be rent-free periods in which you are looking for a tenant to begin your rental income. Every financial product will have a cost and the reason I like mutual funds is that these costs are defined, standardized and have ceilings that cannot be breached. Read Chapter 6 on page 111 for costs. It is possible to buy an index fund for a stamp duty of 0.005 per cent, and an annual expense ratio of less than 20 basis points. The neat costs structure is a plus in my book for mutual funds. Ulips, for example, have an expense ratio but that leaves out the mortality cost—so you need to look at two numbers rather than a single one, making comparison difficult.

A fifth plus is the automatic diversification that a mutual fund scheme provides. A large-cap scheme usually invests in fifty to seventy stocks. The probability of all fifty stocks losing value together (other than due to overall down markets in situations such as a recession or a COVID-19–like calamity) is very low. Some businesses will do well, some won't and, on an average, the returns will be fairly near the index return. But if you choose stocks and do not have the expertise to track the companies and the other global and local events, then it is entirely possible that your selected five to seven stocks all underperform at the same time. By buying carefully across mutual fund categories in the market, you can construct a portfolio that gives you excellent diversification that works to reduce risk and enhance return.

A sixth reason that works in favour of mutual funds is that they can be used to build very diversified portfolios across asset classes and within an asset class. Think of an Indian thali meal—it has some portions of all the needed food components—carbs, proteins, fat, minerals, sweets. You are not just eating roti or bowl after bowl of dal. You are eating a mix. The proportions of the thali will vary according to the age and situation of the person eating. A young seventeen year old might tank up on pooris and aamras (if you have not had pooris and aamras, what can I say!), but a seventy-year-old diabetic might go for bajra roti with some veggies and daal—all in small portions. Mutual funds can be used to build a portfolio that has equity, debt, gold and real estate. Within equity, you can have a portfolio across market caps and across fund manager styles. For example, some fund manager might go for investing in high-growth companies and another might look for higher dividends—both these approaches are called fund manager 'styles'. Within debt, you can build a portfolio with short- and medium-term needs taken care of. To do this on your own, buying individual stocks and bonds will be a huge time-consuming exercise when you construct the portfolio and then managing it will be another big exercise as you will need to track individual products.

I was teaching a class of post-graduate students the basics of mutual funds and had to struggle to get them to stop thinking of investing purely in terms of targeting the highest return. Using investment products for future needs is not just about gathering the highest returns, it is also about the certainty of the money being there, of liquidity, of costs and understanding the risk. Unless you detach from the idea of buying the best performing scheme and 'winning' every year, you will not be able to fully use mutual funds to reach your unique financial goals.

We make the error of going from safe FD investing to taking extreme high risks in day trading, using futures and options and crypto coin investing. There is a middle path of taking reasonable risk to give your long-term money the gift of growth.

You are doing okay if you understand that

1. investing is not just about returns;
2. investing is also about liquidity;
3. investing is about diversification;
4. investing is about costs;
5. investing is about ease of transaction; and
6. investing is about having the money when you need it.

3

THE SAFETY BELT OF REGULATIONS

Rules, like seatbelts, irritate in the normal course, but when things go wrong, they can be savers of life. And money.

Why should you learn about mutual funds? Why not stay with products you know—fixed deposits, insurance policies, real estate, gold? Why do so much work to onboard funds? What makes it such a great investment vehicle? Why not buy the underlying securities directly? To understand this, we need to understand the landscape. We need to see why mutual funds are placed uniquely as a market-linked retail-friendly investment. Stay with me through this because it is not directly related with your portfolio choice, but unless you have faith in the product category and understand the regulations that make it safe from fraud, you will always be open to dumping it during one market crash or during some exotic speculative investment bull market.

Since financial products are invisible, you need a mind-map to understand them before use. Most people are introduced to mutual funds as a high-return alternative to bank deposits. This is a sure way of losing money. We've understood that a mutual fund is just a pipe that connects your savings to various asset classes (equity, debt, gold) and their combinations. Now if this pipe is in the hands of somebody who will divert the money to himself or do something with it that you don't want, there is a problem. It is over decades that the rules of the mutual fund market have been crafted with the aim of reducing various risks for average investors who may not be experts in finance, law and economics.

Scams and stock markets

Investors who have burnt their fingers investing in dubious schemes that promise very high returns know that the biggest risk is somebody running away with your money instead of investing on your behalf or into products that will grow your money. Hoffland Finance, CRB, Saradha, Sahara are all names that are associated with vanished household savings. The advantage with physical investments like real estate and gold is that you can see, wear and live in your investments. Bank FDs are relied on after decades of trust in banking in India, although cooperative banks fail and people lose their money even in bank deposits. The biggest job of a regulator is to build trust in the market so that investors feel safe from the risk of fraud. SEBI has done a good job in making mutual funds fraud free, but it took a long journey, which began with a stock market scam.

1992 was the year of the big stock market scam where a banking loophole became the way to route funds into a huge stock market bubble. A broker called Harshad Mehta became the face of the scam that extended its reach to banks, politicians and stock market movers and shakers. The scam rode on the back of the excitement of the 1991 economic reform in India that was going to unshackle the Indian economy from license raj. Private sector participation was now going to be allowed in many areas including finance. But the headline-grabbing stock market scam exposed the unsophisticated nature of the Indian securities markets and the lack of a regulator to oversee the play of free markets. In the aftermath of the stock market scam, the capital market regulator—the Securities and Exchange Board of India—was born, in 1992, as a statutory body, that is, through an act of Parliament. It was soon called upon to draft the rules of the game for mutual funds.

The mutual fund journey from monopoly to open markets

The Unit Trust of India (UTI) as a public sector mutual fund had been set up in 1963. It had a monopoly market for a full twenty-four years before other public sector entities were allowed in. The learned policymakers and government of those years distrusted the private sector enough to prevent them from coming to the market at all. Not that the public sector unit (PSU) funds covered themselves with any glory. Today, it seems bizarre that attempts to open the mutual fund market to private firms was met with virtue-signalling lectures and speeches that feared the death of household savings at the hands of the evil profit-making private and foreign firms. But, in reality, anytime there is reform in India, the same sets of arguments are put forward by the incumbents that finally lean on citizen interest. And in hindsight, the only mutual fund to have deliberately cheated investors was the old UTI as it kept declaring unrealistic dividends in its flagship scheme Unit 64 that did not reflect the real value of the portfolio and was just an imaginary number. It feels scarily like another humongous retirement-targeting assured-return institution today, but let's not go there.

In 1987, UTI's monopoly was challenged by seven PSU banks and insurance-led institutions including the State Bank of India (SBI), Canara Bank, Life Insurance Corporation (LIC) and General Insurance Corporation of India (GIC). It was early days and the rules of the game were still not established. This lawlessness and lack of road rules would come to bite one of these fund houses much later when the courts held it to account for the guarantee it gave investors. But I run ahead, we are still in the flashback scene! The market was under the Capital Issues (Control) Act, 1947 that determined who would be in charge of capital in socialist India and decided on new issue prices on the stock market. The stock market was a brokers' closed club of incumbents. Like all incumbent-driven institutions, it was expensive, with a trade costing 5 per cent of the value (this is now down to a few basis points) with no transparency on the actual price of the trade since the market was an open outcry system with physical deals rather than the screen-based trading we have now.

The pressure for change was bubbling up to the surface in the nineties and it erupted with the 1991 reform as India stood on the edge of bankruptcy as a country. India had no option but to let go of a system that existed to benefit just a few people at the cost of its citizens in whose name cynically progress, growth and development were tightly stifled. In that reform rush, the Indian capital markets got a full makeover. Policy thought agreed that mutual funds was a good retail vehicle for investors and some road rules were needed before the private sector was allowed in. This gave birth to the first set of formal rules for the mutual fund industry, in 1993. In the same year, Kothari Pioneer set up India's first private sector mutual fund. This was later taken over by Franklin Templeton mutual fund. In 1996, the mutual fund rules changed, but the initial regulations are core even today. All mutual funds, other than the erstwhile monopoly UTI, were brought under these regulations. This exclusion came back to hurt retail investors big time in a few years when UTI's Unit 64 imploded and the government had to intervene. The UTI finally came under the full jurisdiction of SEBI in 2003.

Fraud-proofing the mutual fund industry

Over the years, SEBI has taken its role as the protector of retail investors in mutual funds very seriously. The policy view is that investors into direct stock investors, portfolio management schemes and alternate investment funds are sophisticated and better able to negotiate the market. The level of regulatory oversight needed is lower than that of a pure retail vehicle such as mutual funds. The regulator looks at a very tight regime for mutual funds with almost every action under rules and watch. We need to know this as we try and understand mutual funds better to see what this policy thought translated into and how it aims to prevent fraud and malintention in the deployment of household savings through mutual funds.

The biggest risk in a financial product is fraud, that the entity which collects the money runs away with it—diverting the sum into shell companies and then declaring itself bankrupt. We have to only think of real estate builders who sold the Greater Noida nightmare to remember what fund diversion, ill intent and no regulations can do to household savings. Urban Indians were lured into the dream of owning homes and cheated out of their money by builders who siphoned off the money and left half-completed ghost towns and very angry investors.

Written in the aftermath of scams and taking note of the structures in the rest of the world, the Indian mutual fund has a three-tier structure—sponsor, trust and asset management company (AMC). India has chosen the trust structure so that neither the sponsor nor the AMC can divert the money and vanish. The investor money is held by a trustee company or a board of trustees. This is true as of 2023, but SEBI can change these rules along the way. The trust rules in India are very strict—if found guilty of fraud or misuse of investor funds, the trustees stand to lose their personal assets and can be jailed.

The business is set up by a sponsor who wants to earn a profit from running a mutual fund. For example, the sponsors of SBI Mutual Fund are SBI and Amundi of France, those of HDFC Mutual Fund are HDFC and abrdn InvestmentManagement Ltd. The sponsor of Mirae AMC is the South Korean Mirae Asset Global Investments Co. Ltd.

The sponsors set up a company to manage funds called XYZ asset management company or AMC. The AMC is also called the mutual fund. So, the sponsor sets up the business, the AMC charges a fee for its services and the funds of the investor are held by the trustee company to be deployed in stocks, bonds, gold or any other securities and assets allowed by the regulator.

As a mutual fund investor, you must know the structure of the industry in India to understand that your money is fully safe from the risk of somebody running away with it. In its regulated history in India, no mutual fund has decamped with investors' money. Fund managers can take wrong calls, can try and charge too much and hide costs and performance, front run, and do many things that people who manage other people's money do. But the one thing they cannot do is vanish with your money.

SEBI's seven big steps in investor interest

Starting 1996, SEBI has changed mutual fund regulations incrementally over the years with a view to make the financial product cheaper, more transparent and usable by investors. Since the costs of the product and where they are placed are very important for investor outcomes, it has modified the rules several times to prevent hidden costs, reduce overall costs and make the process clearer. While there are several important rule changes, I will document the big ones that affect your money the most. Many of them were hard fought by the industry to stop them from getting implemented. But SEBI, especially since 2017 when Ajay Tyagi took over as the chairman and the then whole time member Madhabi Puri Buch began working on the industry, the pace and intensity of change has increased. The use of data, big data, analytics and then regulation has been very well done.

2006: SEBI kills the 6 per cent NFO laddoo

SEBI has been proactive, especially when compared to the insurance regulator, in removing hidden costs that are embedded in the price of the financial product.

Investors typically do not ask how much of the money they invest will actually go to work for them and how much is deducted as costs. For example, a traditional insurance policy, as of April 2023, cuts up to 42 per cent of your money before it invests it in the first year.

Before 2006, mutual funds were allowed to charge 6 per cent of a new fund offer (NFO) to the investor. An NFO is the initial issue of a new scheme offered by a mutual fund, and earlier rules allowed for the marketing and distribution costs of such a new offer to be deducted from investors' funds. Suppose an NFO collected Rs 1,000 crore, then Rs 60 crore could be spent out of that on marketing and distribution costs. In addition, there was a front load of 2.25 per cent for every mutual fund scheme investors bought. (Jump ahead to page 112 in Chapter 6 to understand loads better.)

This upfront laddoo or incentive finally ended up with mutual fund agents who extracted between 8 per cent and 9 per cent of the investment from fund houses. Not only were investors losing money in high commissions, but this practice of harvesting commissions was harming them in another way. Agents would sell a high-commission NFO talking up the high returns the market was giving. A bull run gave credence to their sales pitch and investors in 2004–06 piled in. But once they had harvested their commissions, agents would nudge investors to sell and then buy another NFO. Agents made much more money than any investor over this period. Does this not sound like what happens in money-back and endowment polices of life insurance even today? Well, agents there are harvesting more than 40 per cent of your first year premium and are incentivized to keep selling you new policies discarding the old ones. Anyhow, SEBI has been a very proactive regulator, unlike the insurance regulator, and clamped down hard by killing the 6 per cent front commission in 2006. M. Damodaran was the SEBI chief then and I remember a conversation with him on this as I broke the 'churn scam' in *The Indian Express*—asking him why he had left a loophole. He had first stopped open-ended funds from charging the NFO fees, but as the industry rushed to launch close-ended schemes, he stopped this for that category of funds as well in 2008. (Read about open-ended and close-ended funds on page 78, Chapter 5.) He said he had expected better behaviour from the funds and therefore had left the close-ended schemes out earlier! The industry and agents cried blue murder, they said the industry would die. They said investors would lose, but SEBI stood fast behind investor interest. The assets under management were Rs 3.23 trillion in end 2006, which grew to Rs 4.13 trillion by end 2008.

2009: SEBI removed upfront commissions

Till the year 2009, mutual fund investors paid an invisible charge called front load of 2.25 per cent each time they bought a scheme. This money was deducted from investor money by the AMC and given to the agent who sold the product. This means that till August 2009, for every Rs 1 lakh you invested, Rs 2,250 went to the agent as commission and the remaining got invested. In 2009, the then SEBI chairman,

C.B. Bhave, asked a very important question: whose agent is the mutual fund seller? If he is the agent of the mutual fund, then the fund should compensate the agent from his own funds (through the expense ratio) and not deduct investor money. The investor is already paying the AMC through the expense ratio—use that rather than impose another charge. He removed the front load of 2.25 per cent and made Indian mutual funds the first in the world to go no-load. And just as an aside, he also undertook the tough task of trying to curb the huge mis-selling in unit linked insurance policies by staking a regulatory claim on the product. He lost the fight to big business and government interests and did not get an extension to his very fruitful term at SEBI. Big loss for investors. The industry went into a real funk saying that nowhere in the world was the mutual fund a zero upfront commission product. The death of the industry was foretold. But again SEBI held steadfast and said: this front load causes mis-selling and mutual funds are a product for retail investors, so no, this invisible charge goes away. Op-eds were written to say that the industry would die. The narrative grew that investors would lose as the market will shrink. It did, and the assets under management of Rs 6.65 trillion by end 2009, fell over the next few years only to recover and bounce back by 2012.

2013: SEBI allows direct plans

From 1 January 2013, investors got an option to go directly to the scheme and not be forced to go through an agent. Investors who did all the work themselves in choosing and managing their portfolios were forced to pay the trail commission to agents for simply putting the application through to the mutual fund. The direct plan is like opening another door to access the mutual fund, but one that has a lower cost. The costs of commission and distribution were going to be lower in direct plans as compared to regular, agent-sold plans. Remember that the agents' commission is now coming out of the expense ratio since SEBI banned upfront loads. So, ideally, the direct plan-expense ratio should have been between 85 basis points to 1 percentage point lower than the regular plan-expense ratios. But of course, the industry got around that regulation as well, and by 2018, SEBI discovered that there was virtually no difference in the expense ratios of direct and regular plans. Mutual funds were charging direct investors for distribution costs even when there was no intermediary! So, in October 2018, SEBI asked mutual funds to reduce the direct plan-expense ratios to reflect at least the cost of commissions in the regular plans. This has now happened and direct plan-expense ratios are between 25 basis points and 1 percentage point lower than regular plans. By end 2013, the assets under management (AUM) of the mutual fund industry was Rs 8.25 trillion.

2018: SEBI stops upfronting of trail commissions

When you have studied an industry for as long as I have, you begin to see that it will use any loophole, any interpretation of the rule to break it in spirit. After the 2009 regulation that removed front loads in mutual funds, it was hoped that agents would earn trail commission from the expense ratio and this would align their interest with the investor. (Go to page 118 in Chapter 6 to understand trail commission.) As the investor wealth grew, the trail commissions would get larger since they are a percentage of the total portfolio. The agent will be encouraged to sell a fund that works for the investors and encourage an equity investor to stay long term, since each year he stands to earn about 1 per cent of the total assets under management as a trail commission. This worked for some time but then some sharp shooters began to upfront the trail commission for the first year. This meant that mutual funds would pay the agents at the beginning of the year from their own profits and capital rather than wait till the end of the year. Then agents pushed for upfronting for two years and then for three, and then five years. By 2017, some large distributors were arm-twisting AMCs to fork over 5 per cent of the investment over the next five years at the point of sale. SEBI first capped the upfronting to 1 per cent of the investment and then banned it fully in 2018. Any upfront commission is an invitation to agents to mis-sell and churn and the repeated regulatory action has made the product more and more mis-selling unfriendly. But, again, the public debate was not about investors, but about the loss of livelihood of mutual fund agents. Of the industry going out of business. Again, they said the industry would die. They said investors would go to unregulated parts of the market! The assets under management were at Rs 22.86 trillion by end 2018.

2019: Reducing expense ratios on mutual funds

SEBI reduced the expense ratio limits for the industry in 2019 to take note of the much larger assets under management. (Read Chapter 6, page 121 for a better understanding of this reduction and why it matters to you.) As a mutual fund grows, its fixed costs remain almost constant and there is not that much more cost as the money under management rises. Theoretically, the expense ratio for large funds should see a sharp fall, but that did not happen. Funds found ways to use the higher expense ratios on very large AUMs to benefit agents or book huge profits rather than pass on the benefit to investors. SEBI again swung into action and reduced the overall expenses on both equity and debt funds. For equity funds, the maximum a regular plan can charge came down from 1.75 per cent to 1.05 per cent for schemes with assets higher than Rs 50,000 crore. For debt funds, the number is 0.80 per cent. Direct plans are cheaper after excluding the trail commission costs of sellers. The overall costs of the investor have gone down. The AUM at the end of 2019 stood at Rs 26.54 trillion.

2020: Making funds 'true to label'

It is important for investors to get a product they buy, especially when the product is invisible. In an invisible product, the labels take on a larger-than-life importance for investors and need to be 'true to label'. For example, if the cake label says egg-free, then there really must be no eggs in the cake. Mutual funds were mixing higher risk funds in schemes that were labelled to show them as lower risk schemes and this was misleading investors. As the industry grew in size, SEBI felt the need to bring some order in the way mutual funds were labelled. In the October 2017 regulations, SEBI defined large-, mid- and small-cap stocks so that the funds investing in them would reflect the underlying security better. The regulator also tried to improve labelling by preventing funds from using the word 'opportunity' instead of 'risk' in certain categories such as debt funds that took a higher credit risk. (Skip ahead to page 143 in Chapter 7 to understand credit risk better.) For example, the credit opportunity fund was re-labelled as 'credit risk' fund. The category offers a way for risk-seeking debt fund investors who don't mind buying lower credit quality paper, a way to target higher return. But calling it an opportunity did not reflect the huge risk that investors would take. So SEBI re-labelled these as credit risk funds.

In the same year, SEBI also categorized open-ended mutual funds into thirty-six categories with well-defined norms on what each can invest in. For example, a multi-cap scheme must invest in large-, mid- and small-cap stocks with at least 25 per cent in each cap. Each fund house was allowed to have only one scheme in each category. By 2020, the number of categories was thirty-seven as the regulator allowed one more equity category on industry demand—a flexi-cap fund.

Read more about this on page 50 in Chapter 4. Understand what the regulator has tried to do—make choosing easier by limiting the number of categories, defining what can be put in each category and then allowing each fund house to have only one scheme in the category. The AUM at the end of 2020 was Rs 31.02 trillion.

2021: Marking risk clearly through a dynamic Risk-o-Meter

To give investors a way to measure risk of a scheme, SEBI took the existing Risk-o-Meter that marked risk in a stagnant manner and turned it into a dynamic one. Read more on the Risk-o-Meter and how to use it on page 154 in Chapter 7. The fund houses are supposed to evaluate the risk of the portfolio each month and update the risk reading on the Association of Mutual Funds in India (AMFI) site. Once a year, they need to report how many times the risk reading changed over the year. This is especially relevant in debt funds and is a great tool that should be used by you to evaluate if you should invest in a fund whose risk rating bounces around too much. The AUM stood at Rs 37.73 trillion at the end of 2021.

Looking at the SEBI-induced changes and ever-tighter regulations, it is fair to say that this is certainly not an industry that has either died or not served investors. The voices of protest on each regulatory action have reduced as the evidence that crafting a product that works for investors actually works for the industry has become stronger over the years. These are just some of the big changes I have documented here, but the work of a regulator is never over when it comes to the financial sector. I anticipate on going regulation on costs with trail commission coming under the lens soon. I also expect more rules around index funds in a few years.

When you see the mar gaye, lut gaye stories in the press when SEBI does its next round of reform, come back and read this chapter and remember it is being done in your interest. As a mutual fund investor, you need to know how easy it is for a fund manager to find loopholes in rules and do their own thing. From inter-scheme transfer of securities that do not benefit the non-flagship schemes to interpreting long-term bonds as short term on a technicality to qualify the bond for a short-duration fund, the industry has done it all. But rather than put you off, the constant cat-and-mouse game played by SEBI and the industry should actually build confidence. At least all this is in the notice of the regulator, which does something about it and changes rules constantly to keep the investors' interest foremost.

Other regulators are very passive and simply do not care to take action on adequate meaningful disclosures or rules and practices that hurt investors. For example, the life insurance regulator allows life insurance firms to deduct your entire first premium if you do not pay the second one. If after five premiums you decide not to pay the sixth, the insurance industry is allowed by the regulator to eat up half your capital! We're not talking returns here. This is a loss of principal for changing your mind.

The SEBI rules make Indian mutual funds less prone to mis-selling because they have removed most of the conflict of interest of the agent selling it to you by removing all manner of front commissions, thus ensuring that under-the-bonnet changes made the product far safer than before. Disclosures are good and there are plenty of independent analysts that give you details on performance, expense ratios and portfolios in an easy-to-understand manner. But remember that the financial sector is always a few steps ahead and over time, malpractice begins to build. Ideally stay with fund houses that are known for good management practices and putting investor interest ahead. As I say often, investing is not just about earning the highest return over one or two years, but having an investing partner over your lifetime.

From the next chapter, we begin the process of choosing a mutual fund scheme. Instead of giving you a readymade meal, I want you to create your own so that you can continue the process over your investing lifetime. A curated meal today might not suit you tomorrow. But if you know the steps to the decision making, then you can truly do it yourself. This is not an easy process, but do it once, however long it takes—it is a one-time hard effort that will give you dividends for the rest of your investing life. Onwards to the work ahead!

As an individual investor, we need a path that has rules of the game that work in our favour rather than for the benefit of just the industry and the agent. A good regulator that has consistently worked in investor interest makes mutual funds a great choice for an average household in India.

You are doing okay if you understand that mutual funds

1. are free from the risk of fraud;
2. are not free from the risk of markets doing badly;
3. are not free from fund managers taking wrong calls;
4. have costs that are defined, and easy to understand and compare;
5. are true to label—you mostly get what you are buying; and
6. have no front commissions in the price of the product.

4

THE CHOICE SET

Some choice is better than no choice. But, paradoxical to conventional wisdom, less choice is better than too many options when it comes to taking action.

There is a sequence in the movie *English Vinglish* where Shashi (played by Sridevi) is so intimidated by the choices in a Manhattan café that she has a breakdown. I feel like that sometimes when hit by a barrage of choices in a café too. What kind of coffee (ten choices), with what flavour (seven choices), with milk or not. If milk, what kind of milk (the only thing not on offer seems to be camel milk—seriously, it is a thing!), hereortogo? Will you have something to eat? What, no! *Hey bhagwan*! Just want a coffee, dude.

While coffee choices are important, they don't have far-reaching consequences on your future, like the decisions on investing. Our future selves and their lifestyles depend upon the choices we make today. And when mutual funds are our chosen vehicle of investment, we need to understand all the choices of fund options and how we enter and exit them. I will say this again and again, at the risk of irritating you, understand this once and you are sorted with your big money decisions for the rest of your life. You will need to make incremental choices and not the big, scary ones that we are trying to work through now.

Choice overload is something new for us in India. Those of us born before the new millennium grew up in a supply-starved country. Just having choice was a luxury, so what if it was between few options with poor quality and service. Then came 1991 and the shackles around business were loosened. Market forces took over and Indians got choice. From two car companies to more than two dozen. From long lines of waiting for a telephone connection, to broadband on demand from competing companies. We need only a trip to the supermarket right now to see the sheer volume of choice available. I was looking for a TV to replace my trusted but tired twelve-year-old set that needed finally to be allowed to die. The screen would warm up slowly and it would take ten-fifteen minutes for the line between the top half and the bottom half to disappear for me to get a full screen view. When that time became one hour and more, I knew it was time. Time to let go. Other than laziness, one reason for not allowing a merciful death earlier was the sheer fear of choosing another one. In these twelve years, the choice set of TVs had expanded so much that I did not even know where to begin. This tyranny of choice (that is actually a thing with papers and such written on it!) was leading me to a decision paralysis.

Did you hear of the famous jam study? Economist and choice theory expert at the Columbia Business School Sheena Iyengar, in a unique study in the year 2000, established that more choice led to fewer buying decisions and less satisfaction. The experiment went like this: In an upmarket store in America, shoppers were invited to taste a variety of jams ahead of purchase. The counter rotated the choice of jams every hour—one hour, there was on offer twenty-four flavours of jam and another hour, there were only six. Given the premise that more choice is better, we would imagine that the twenty-four jam counter would see more action and therefore sales, right? Wrong! The study found that the larger jam counter attracted 60 per cent of the shoppers present in the store, the smaller jam counter got just 40 per cent to stop to sample. The greater choice counter saw an average of 1.5 jams being tasted and the smaller choice saw 1.4 jams being tasted. But when it came to sales, the twenty-four jam counter saw just 3 per cent of the shoppers buying, while 30 per cent of shoppers bought when they stopped by the six jam counter. Not only did the larger choice counter see fewer sales, subsequent research showed that those shoppers displayed less satisfaction with their choices. The idea that there was a better jam that was not bought weighed heavier when there was a greater choice set than when there were fewer options.

Think of why we tend to postpone our investment decisions—there is just too much choice in the market. And worse, a bottle of jam can be discarded with no long-term impact if you finally don't like the flavour, but investment decisions have lifetime impacts—the consequences of wrong decisions will cost you money. Therefore, we look for the perfect investment product with the best possible return and, since perfection is a momentary space that we occupy and not a continuum, we fail. When we choose, we use the one metric we know about market-linked financial products—high return—to evaluate and choose. But when we ignore other attributes such as risk, liquidity, tax impact, cost and exit options—to name a few—we end up making wrong choices.

The mutual fund choice set

There are over 1,200 mutual fund schemes with option combinations that take the choices to be made to over 10,000. You will lose the game if you begin by choosing a scheme without a choice matrix in mind. When you go to choose a car, where do you begin? You choose a category first. Hatchback, sedan, SUV, luxury is your first cut of category choice, isn't it? Then you can go deeper on specifications within the category. We can do the same with mutual funds. We choose a category and then we choose a scheme from it.

It was in 2016 that SEBI found that mutual fund companies were launching similar schemes that were confusing investors. For example, one fund house had four large-cap schemes with different names. I remember getting a portfolio analysis for the newspaper where I edited the personal finance pages and found a 90 per cent overlap of stocks in the four schemes. Another had a balanced fund that had mid-cap stocks in it.

SEBI found that funds were not being true to label or the stocks and bonds in the portfolio did not represent the investment theme that was sold to investors. Think of it this way—you are at a bus station and there are buses ready to go with the destination written on the bus front and back windows. You are in Delhi and the buses are going to Noida, Gurugram and Faridabad. You get into the Gurugram bus as you were planning to visit Cyber City and meet a friend.

Cyber City, by the way, is this happening place in Gurugram with lovely hangout spots. And if you do go there, you must visit.... Got it, back to mutual funds. This is a book on funds. Sorry! So, we're trying to get to Gurugram and the label on the bus says Gurugram, but the bus driver has something else in mind and you find yourself being driven to Faridabad. Apart from a very angry friend who missed you in that lovely lounge in Cyber City, you really did not want to be in Faridabad. Absurd, right, to bring you to another place while your destination label said something else? Well, that is what was happening in the mutual fund industry—the stocks and bonds in the portfolios sometimes had no relation to the label displayed, misleading investors and causing them usually to take far more risk than they wanted to.

SEBI put order in the market by doing two things. One, it specified thirty-seven categories for open-ended funds with very well-defined portfolio characteristics. (We will understand open-ended funds later in Chapter 5, page 78.) Two, it allowed each fund house to have only one scheme in each category. Close-ended funds were outside this categorization—more on this on page 78, Chapter 5. The categories were decided keeping in mind investor needs for a well-diversified portfolio and their money requirements at different time periods in the future.

The debate on how to solve the too many me-too schemes issue had been an ongoing one, and once, as a member of SEBI's mutual fund committee from 2009 to 2021, I remember that I suggested the one-bucket-one-scheme idea. I then wrote it as a column in *Mint*.[1] A consultative subcommittee process that took more than six months finally resulted in the thirty-seven categories across five groups. There are eleven categories in equity, sixteen in debt, six in hybrid, two in solution-oriented and two in others.

Table 4.1

Thirty-seven mutual fund categories for open-ended funds					
	Equity	Debt	Hybrid	Solution oriented	Other schemes
1	Multi-cap	Overnight	Conservative hybrid	Retirement fund	Index/ ETFs
2	Large-cap	Liquid	Balanced/ aggressive hybrid	Children's fund	FoF (overseas/ domestic)
3	Large- and mid-cap	Ultra-short duration	Dynamic asset allocation/ balanced advantage		

Thirty-seven mutual fund categories for open-ended funds					
	Equity	Debt	Hybrid	Solution oriented	Other schemes
4	Mid-cap	Low duration	Multi-asset allocation		
5	Small-cap	Money market	Arbitrage		
6	Dividend yield	Short duration	Equity savings		
7	Value/contra	Medium duration			
8	Focused	Medium to long duration			
9	Sectoral/thematic	Long duration			
10	ELSS	Dynamic bond			
11	Flexi-cap	Corporate bond			
12		Credit risk			
13		Banking and PSU			
14		Gilt			
15		Gilt with ten year constant duration			
16		Floater			

You need to belt up now for a deep dive into categories and their best-fit uses. I am trying to make you independent in choosing funds for all time to come—so if you crack this once, you will never ask questions like 'is this a good time to buy mutual funds?'

The eleven equity categories

Table 4.2

Eleven equity categories			
	Equity	Scheme characteristics	Type of scheme
1	Multi-cap	Min 65% of total assets in equity and related instruments	Min of 25% each in large-, mid- and small-cap stocks
2	Large-cap	Min 80% of total assets in large-cap equity and related instruments	Invests predominantly in large-cap stocks
3	Large- and mid-cap	Min 35% of total assets each in large- and mid-cap stocks and related instruments	Invests in both large- and mid-cap stocks
4	Mid-cap	Min 65% of total assets in mid-cap equity and related instruments	Invests predominantly in mid-cap stocks
5	Small-cap	Min 65% of total assets in small-cap equity and related instruments	Invests predominantly in small-cap stocks

Eleven equity categories			
	Equity	Scheme characteristics	Type of scheme
6	Dividend yield	Min 65% of total assets in dividend-yielding stocks	Invests predominantly in dividend-yielding stocks
7	Value/contra	Min 65% of total assets in value stocks or in a contrarian investment strategy	Invests predominantly in value stocks or follows a contrarian investment strategy
8	Focused	Min 65% of total assets in a maximum of thirty stocks	Funds have to indicate cap strategy—max thirty stocks in multi/large/mid/small stocks
9	Sectoral/thematic	Min 80% of total assets in a particular sector or theme	Fund has to specify sector or theme
10	ELSS	Min 80% of assets in specified equity and related instruments	Scheme has a three-year lock-in and gets the 80C deduction benefit as in FY24
11	Flexi-cap	Min 65% of total assets in equity and related instruments	Invests dynamically across large/mid/small stocks according to fund manager calls

If you don't remember what equity as an asset class means, go and do a quick recap in *Let's Talk Money* in Chapter 8. You need equity in your portfolio to give your money long-term growth. You need some, and not all, of the eleven categories. But, to remove what you don't need, we need to go through the list and understand what part of the market or investing style each straddle.

We can divide the stocks in the market into three buckets based on their market cap. Market cap is just the number of stocks multiplied by the market price to give an indication of the size of the company rather than using turnover or profit. Large-cap stocks are the first 100 stocks listed on the stock exchanges in India. Mid-cap stocks lie between the 101st stock and the 250th stock. Small-caps are 251st stock onwards in terms of market cap. Large-cap stocks are typically of large well-established companies that are in the mature phase of their growth. Investors usually use large-caps to give return stability to their equity portfolio. Mid-caps are fast-growing companies that have potential to one day become a large-cap if they can keep growing. These are used by investors to take higher risk in their equity portfolio to target higher returns than large-cap stocks. Small-cap are the riskiest part of the market, but have the potential to give very high returns. But small-caps are volatile in the short run and can yo-yo between being the top performer category for the year and the bottom performer in a subsequent year. You need to be able to hold a consistent fund and onto your emotions for a decade to see their magic.

So, we have the three basic categories—large-, mid- and small-cap funds. We now know a little bit about their risk and return faces. Next are the three cross-cap categories—multi-cap, flexi-cap and large- and mid-cap. Remember that SEBI's exercise took place when there were already thousands of crores of investor money across categories. Flexi-cap and large- and mid-cap were two such categories. The flexi-cap category allows the fund manager to invest anywhere in the market across market-caps, the only restriction is that 65 per cent of the assets must be in equity. The fund manager can move dynamically between large-, mid- and small-cap stocks and this gives huge flexibility to the fund manager to predict the next cap cycle and time it to harvest the best returns for investors. If fund managers were really good at predicting the next winning cycle, this category of funds would have outperformed all the categories in equity, I imagine. But when we look at the evidence, this outperformance is not seen. On an average, the flexi-cap funds remain over-invested in large-caps.

A multi-cap fund is more true to label as it has an investing floor built into the category mandate. The fund manager must invest at least 25 per cent of AUM in each of the three market caps. This typically works out to be 50 per cent in large-caps, 25 per cent in mid-caps and 25 per cent in small-caps. This category does not have enough performance history for us to judge how they have done. My hunch is that they will outperform the flexi-cap category since the fund managers will be forced to pick winning stocks out of the mid- and small-cap buckets, that have higher return potential but come with a higher risk.

Remember that it is far safer for the fund manager to have a large-cap bias since that is a lower risk strategy. But if I, as an investor, want to do off-roading and get that burst of adrenaline, why would I take a tram? If I am buying a fund that invests across market caps, it should actually go ahead and do that rather than stay safe in the large-cap bucket. The fund categories are meant for you to match your investment portfolio needs and investing style to offer a good fit.

The next three categories have limited value in most retail portfolios—these are dividend yield, focused and value/contra funds. A dividend yield fund aims to invest in stocks that give you high dividends. Over the past ten years, this category has hugged an average large-cap fund showing that it gives a near-index return. You might as well buy a low-cost index fund rather than this category. You can read more about index funds and how to use them in Chapter 11 on page 218.

Focused funds offer to stay within a restriction of a maximum of thirty stocks across any market cap or style and give the investor the benefit of a very tightly focused portfolio. Remember that the top 100 stocks in the large-cap bucket range from a Reliance Industries at a market cap of almost Rs 16 lakh crore as on 6 April 2023 which is almost 30 times bigger than a Schaeffler India with a market cap of just over Rs 47,280 crore. A fund manager may want to run a thirty-stock portfolio that picks from the bottom of the large-cap pile or thirty stocks from the top of the mid-cap pile. I hope you notice that the bottom of the large-cap picks are riskier in a large-cap fund than the top thirty stocks in the same category and the top thirty stocks in a mid-cap fund are lower risk than the bottom thirty in the same category. The fund manager can define her style of investing and attempt to target a higher return. The history of this category does not show consistent return over time that justifies the higher risk of stock concentration. For a mature seasoned investor, this category could be used for targeting a higher return than the category offers, but definitely not for a newbie investor. It is just needless risk that does not seem to be worth the ride over time.

Then come the value/contra funds. Fund houses can choose one of the two—either have a value fund or a contra fund. Mutual funds wanted both! SEBI's logic for one category for both is that a value strategy is a contrarian one—so where is the need for a different category? Actually, we can extend that logic to say that a fund manager in the other categories is also trying to identify stocks that are going to show appreciation over time. The growth vs value debate was put to rest by Warren Buffett (if you don't know who he is, you've been living under a rock!) when he wrote in a letter to shareholders of Berkshire Hathaway Inc back in 2000: 'Market commentators and investment managers who glibly refer to "growth" and "value" styles as contrasting approaches to investment are displaying their ignorance, not their sophistication. Growth is simply a component, usually a plus, sometimes a minus, in the value equation.'

The next category is ELSS or equity linked saving scheme. This is a scheme notified by the government to be eligible for the Section 80C benefit. (Read more on page 169 in Chapter 8 on taxes.) There is a three-year lock-in before you can redeem these funds. A small piece of statistics here—the average ten-year annual return for the ELSS category is almost 15 per cent. The worst fund gave 12 per cent and the best 21 per cent as on 6 April 2023.

This is a great category for those wanting the deduction, much better than the toxic endowment policies that work only for the agent and the insurance firms and not for you as an investor. The winning combination is a term-insurance plan whose premium gets you the tax break plus ELSS for investment.

The last category is sectoral/thematic funds and this is for the mature mutual fund investor who already has a basic portfolio in place. This is not the first or even the second or third equity fund you buy. This is a category that allows the fund manager to follow a sector or a theme. A sector can be information technology, infrastructure, pharma and so on. A theme could be consumption, ethics, business cycle, special situations and more. While a sector fund, such as pharma or auto, can be a tactical investment for somebody who knows and understands the sector deeply, thematic funds are just well-dressed large-cap funds at heart. Best for a new investor to stay well away.

From these eleven categories, six are useful for you: large-cap, mid-cap, small-cap, large- and mid-cap, ELSS and multi-cap funds. Just ignore the rest. In Chapters 9 and 10 we will see how to use some of these categories to build portfolios. But for now, we have shortlisted the categories from which we will choose our equity funds. Remember that I am including index funds on the Sensex and Nifty within the category of large-cap funds. Large-cap funds have mostly stopped generating a return that is higher than the benchmark and for most portfolios, instead of an active large-cap, a Sensex or Nifty 50 index fund is a better choice. More on this later. Read about benchmarks on page 131 in Chapter 6.

The sixteen debt categories

Table 4.3

Sixteen debt categories		
	Debt	Scheme characteristics
1	Overnight	Invests in overnight securities with a maturity of one day
2	Liquid	Invests in debt and money market instruments with a residual maturity up to ninety-one days
3	Ultra-short duration	Invests in debt and money market instruments such that Macaulay duration of portfolio is between three and six months
4	Low duration	Invests in debt and money market instruments such that Macaulay duration of portfolio is between six and twelve months
5	Money market	Invests in money market instruments with maturity up to one year

Sixteen debt categories		
	Debt	Scheme characteristics
6	Short duration	Invests in debt and money market instruments such that Macaulay duration of portfolio is between one and three years
7	Medium duration	Invests in debt and money market instruments such that Macaulay duration of portfolio is between three and four years
8	Medium to long duration	Invests in debt and money market instruments such that Macaulay duration of portfolio is between four and seven years
9	Long duration	Invests in debt and money market instruments such that Macaulay duration of portfolio is longer than seven years
10	Dynamic bond	Invests across durations
11	Corporate bond	Invests min 80% of assets in AA+ and above corporate bonds
12	Credit risk	Invests min 65% of assets in below highest rated bonds
13	Banking and PSU	Invests min 80% of assets in banks, PSU, PFI instruments
14	Gilt	Invests min 80% of assets in G-secs across maturities
15	Gilt ten-year constant duration	Invests min 80% of assets in G-secs so that Macaulay duration of portfolio is ten years
16	Floater	Invests min 65% of total assets in floating rate instruments

Debt funds invest in debt securities like government bonds, corporate bonds and deposits. Debt products are meant to give liquidity and safety to a portfolio. Ideally, we do not use debt products to take too much risk. I will repeat this again and again: a good investment is not just about the highest return, but also about low costs, liquidity and having access to the money when needed. I was recently asked by somebody very senior in the regulatory space: liquid funds are giving 7 per cent, should I move my money to that? I could not speak for a full thirty seconds. That person should have known better than to try and market time-liquid funds!

We do not use liquid fund to target large returns. We use liquid funds to have money available in the next three months. We need to fully discard this harvest-the-highest-return mindset and work with matching our money needs with the debt categories.

Debt is a difficult asset class to understand for most investors and the chances of going wrong are higher than equity. In equity funds, we know that there is risk. In debt funds, investors seem to believe that these are risk free. That is also how many fund houses have promoted this asset class. But they are certainly not risk free. You need to see the face of risk and then choose from categories that work for you, rather than chase return. SEBI has spent close to two years redoing the entire debt fund landscape to make it much safer for investors. Some categories are now very real alternatives to bank savings and fixed deposits. Take a coffee break and come back—this is not easy stuff to understand. But understand you must because the rest of your money journey depends on getting the basics right. Even if you work with a financial planner, it is good to know what he or she is actually doing.

The first category is an overnight fund, which holds debt securities such as treasury bills and other more technical names that we don't need to get into here. What we need to know is that the average maturity of these bonds is one day. This means that all the bonds in this overnight fund will mature or pay back the principal along with the interest on the next day. We will understand the risk in a bond fund better in Chapter 7, but at the moment what we must know is that the closer to today the maturity of the bond is, the lower is the risk of an interest rate change and the further away from today the maturity is, the higher is the risk of such a change. So, overnight bond funds carry very little risk and give returns that are usually better than a savings deposit. These are useful for corporate treasuries and super-high net worth people, and have very little use in an average retail portfolio.

The next one is called liquid fund, which has bonds that will typically mature in three months. It might even have bonds that were launched many years ago, but now have just three months left for maturity. This is a category that aims to keep your principal safe and allows you to target a corpus needed in the next three months. Typically used to park funds that are needed in the next two-to-four months for goals including paying home down-payment, bills towards education or a vacation. We do not want to take risk with this money and will only go for low risk on the Risk-o-Meter. Read page 154 in Chapter 7 for more on this risk marker.

Ultra-short-duration funds are best for an investment horizon of three to six months. Duration is just a technical financial concept that is used to predict the change in bond prices when interest rates change. When interest rates go up, bond prices fall. Think it through—you are a fund manager holding bonds that give a 6 per cent interest, but due to a hike in policy rates, the new bonds are being issued at 8 per cent. You will want to sell the 6 per cent bonds and buy the 8 per cent ones for a higher return. Other fund managers will think the same thoughts and go to market to sell. When there is an excess of supply, the price will fall. The reverse happens when interest rates fall—therefore, interest rates and bond prices are inversely related. Duration is just a mathematical formula (no, you don't need to know it or calculate it, you just need to know about it) that predicts the extent to which bond prices might change (down or up) for every 1 per cent change (up or down) in interest rates.

Low-duration funds are good for money needs that will occur between six months to a year later than today. The next category, money market funds, are useful for money needs that are within the next year.

Short-duration funds, for money needs that are between one and three years away. Medium-duration category, for needs that are three-to-four years later. Medium-to-long duration for targeting a corpus that is between four-to-seven years from today. Long duration for a holding period of more than seven years. These categories are trying to match your holding period and money needs to bond fund categories. Notice that these debt fund categories are aimed at making it easy for you to match your holding period of the investment to the bond portfolio. You don't want to be holding a long-tenor bond when you want the money in three months. By ensuring that the bonds held in each category are true to their label, SEBI has tried to make it easy for investors to choose the category they need.

I like to use debt funds for money needs that are up to three or four years away. After that I prefer to use a mix of debt and equity. For near-term needs, I want certainty of the money being there when I want it. For my longer term needs, I use equity. But, let's go through the categories just to know what is out there and why we don't need most of them.

A dynamic bond fund allows the fund manager to have bonds that mature at different times—it is across durations. This fund will usually show up as a moderate risk on the Risk-o-Meter. Best avoided by new bond fund investors as the fund manager risk is high in this case. (See page 156 in Chapter 7 for more on this kind of risk.)

Investors usually get attracted to corporate bond funds and credit risk funds since they sometimes give returns that are very high. In fact, in 2015, credit risk funds outperformed all other categories of mutual fund and asset classes. To understand these mutual funds, we need to understand a concept called credit risk. This is the risk of the borrower not giving the due interest and principal back to the lender.

When mutual funds buy corporate bond securities, they in effect lend money in return for interest and the promise to pay the principal back. When the government borrows, it does so at the lowest rates of interest because its credit risk is zero, which means that the government (at least in India) will always pay back its lenders. But imagine a high-risk sector like real estate. Why do you think real estate firms float deposits and issue bonds with very high rates of interest? Because their risk of default (not paying back interest and principal) is high. Debt funds that invest in non-government bonds are called corporate bond funds. These are meant for debt fund investors who are seeking a higher return than the categories mentioned above. The investor will have to match their ideal holding period to that of the scheme they choose out of all the ones on offer. These are typically ranked low to moderate on the Risk-o-Meter.

Credit risk funds invest in bonds that have a credit rating of AA and below. What is AA? It is a credit rating. What is that? Since it is very difficult for an investor to judge the credit risk of a bond, the global best practice is to get credit rating agencies to give a rating to each bond. For example, a triple A rating means the highest probability of the bond returning both interest and principal on time. A bond with a rating of D is essentially a junk bond—these will have to offer very high rates of interest to see any buyers in the market. Fund managers who want to play the high-risk, high-return game like to invest in the bonds with lower credit rating. SEBI decided to change the name of the category from credit opportunities to credit risk so that retail investors are better able to understand that the potential for a higher return is accompanied by much higher risk.

My very simple advice to you is this: why take the risk that is sometimes higher than the risk of equity in the debt part of your portfolio? Leave this category for those who understand the debt funds well enough and have the stomach to take the risk in the safer part of their portfolio.

Gilt funds invest only in government securities of both the Centre and the states. Since they are of a longer maturity, they carry interest rate risk, but no credit risk—risky for holding in the short term but fairly good returns over a longer holding period. The ten-year plus holding period funds are called gilt ten-year constant duration. But I prefer to use provident fund (PF) and public provident fund (PPF) as long-term debt instruments rather than debt funds. I have certainty of return and both are tax free even at exit. Debt funds now pay tax that is not different from a bank FD. (Look at page 176 in Chapter 8 to find out how much.)

The banking and public sector undertaking (PSU) fund invests in bond paper of banks, public sector units and public financial institutions. Given that these have much lower credit risk, your risk comes more from interest rate changes. The fact that credit risk is low and interest rate risk can be managed makes this category a good one for use for investors who want to target money that will be used in the medium time frame of three to five years. It is good to stay with low to moderate on the Risk-o-Meter with this category of funds.

Floater funds is a category that invests in bonds with interest tied to a benchmark that can move up or down. The returns will float up when rates in the economy rise and float down when the reverse happens. Seen as a lower risk way of investing in debt funds, it still leaves the investor open to credit risk. Investors must also know how to time the markets to best use this category of funds.

My advice: use debt funds on the shorter end of the holding period for needs that are within three to four years. Leave the use of other categories to the debt fund experts or if you are working with a planner, use these for a rise in the overall return on the portfolio.

The six hybrid categories

Table 4.4

Six hybrid categories			
	Hybrid	Scheme characteristics	Type of scheme
1	Conservative hybrid	Invests between 10% and 25% of assets in equity and related instruments and between 75% and 90% in debt instruments	Predominantly a debt fund
2	Balanced hybrid	Invests between 40% and 60% of assets in debt and equity each with no arbitrage	A balanced fund between debt and equity

Six hybrid categories			
	Hybrid	Scheme characteristics	Type of scheme
	Aggressive hybrid	Invests between 65% and 80% of assets in equity and related instruments and between 20% and35% in debt instruments	Predominantly an equity fund
3	Dynamic asset allocation or balanced advantage	Invests dynamically between equity and debt	Go anywhere fund between debt and equity
4	Multi-asset allocation	Invests a min 10% of assets in at least three asset classes each	Can invest in equity, debt, gold, cash, commodities
5	Arbitrage	Invests a min 65% of assets in equity and related instruments with an arbitrage strategy	Makes money out of the difference in spot and future prices, debt like returns, but taxed like equity
6	Equity savings	Invests a min 65% in equity and related instruments and a min of 10% in debt of assets, with arbitrage strategy	Equity, arbitrage and debt scheme

These are a blend of equity and debt in various combinations aimed at specific investor profiles. Like the other categories, it is good to match each of these categories to your needs, age, stage and risk capacity. More on this in Chapter 12 where I build some model portfolios based on risk capacity levels.

Some history here: most of the schemes in these categories were called balanced funds till the categorization change happened. The word balanced means equal. SEBI, in its desire to make funds true to label changed the way these funds are named to make investors better understand what they are buying. A balanced fund with 75 per cent equity was certainly not balanced, therefore, the change in name to hybrid.

A conservative hybrid fund is a debt fund with a little bit of equity that gives a good mix of stability and some growth. Schemes need to have between 75 per cent to 90 per cent in debt and between 10 per cent to 25 per cent in equity. The average category return over the long run will be higher than most low-risk debt categories (excluding credit risk and corporate bonds, for example) but lower than a broad market equity index return. These are good for income-seeking investors who have a large corpus in place and want to milk it for regular income. (For options that can be used to get a regular income, see Chapter 5, page 89.) Many investors use a systematic withdrawal plan (SWP) to draw a return from these funds. (Turn to page 106 in Chapter 5 to understand SWPs and to page 178 in Chapter 8 to understand the tax impact.)

AMCs can choose to have one or the other of the two similar options in the next category—balanced hybrid or aggressive hybrid. A balanced hybrid fund must have between 40 per cent and 60 per cent in debt and equity. This was going to be 50 per cent each but the fund houses wanted some elbow room and since the arguments went on for a long time, SEBI gave in and allowed them to have 10 per cent leeway on either side of 50 per cent! The kind of chindi mol bhaav that goes on over most regulatory changes between the industry and the regulator has to be seen to be believed! This category is a neither-here-nor-there category since there is a fair bit of equity but the tax advantage of an equity fund of lower capital gains tax does not go to them since an equity fund needs to be at least 65 per cent in equity to qualify for the tax treatment. Read page 177 in Chapter 8 for taxes on equity funds.

One risk is that the Risk-o-Meter will not catch the quality of bond portfolio easily. The blend of equity makes the risk metric for most funds as moderately high, but we need to see what the risk metrics of the bond portfolio is on both interest rate risk and credit risk. For this you will need to go deeper and read Chapter 7 that explains this risk.

The other option for fund houses in this category is aggressive hybrid where the equity part of the portfolio must be between 65 per cent and 80 per cent and the debt part must be between 20 per cent and 35 per cent. This category gets the equity tax treatment and is placed to give returns that are very similar to large-cap returns but with lower risk since there is a cushion of debt in this blended fund—a good option for a risk-averse first-time equity investor who wants a safety belt of some debt in the portfolio. An alternate to this category is a lower cost equity broadmarket index fund. More on this when we examine index funds later in this chapter. An immediate advantage of these funds is that each time there is rebalancing between equity and debt, you don't need to pay tax. Read more on this in Chapter 8 on taxation of mutual funds.

A popular category is balanced advantage fund, also called the dynamic asset allocation fund. This is a go-anywhere fund where the fund manager can move between debt and equity without any limits on either. The idea is that the fund manager is better able to judge the potentially winning asset class and will move money ahead of a bull run in either to harvest a higher return. The fund manager risk (the risk of the fund manager not performing well) is very high in this category and the returns have been typically lower than a large-cap fund, though higher than a conservative or balanced hybrid fund. For a low-risk investor, this is not a great category to choose as the wrong fund and manager can give you suboptimal returns for a much higher cost than a simple equity broadmarket index fund.

A multi-asset allocation fund allows the fund manager to invest across three asset classes at least with a minimum of 10 per cent in each. Funds invest across equity, debt, commodities, cash, gold and real estate—a high-risk category that leaves a lot in the hands of the fund manager to get the asset allocation calls right. Each fund will use its own allocation between any three asset classes it chooses, making comparisons difficult. The category average has done worse than a broad market index fund over a three, five and ten-year period.

Arbitrage funds play on the price difference between spot and futures markets. A spot market is where the securities are traded today and a futures markets is one where the trade (delivery and payment) will happen in the future. You need to understand two things about this category. One, you will get an average return that is above the liquid fund or ultra-short-duration funds and not equity returns. These are sold as equity funds that are safe, but what you are not told is that you should not expect long-term growth. These are an alternative to a debt fund for a holding period of less than a year. Two, because these are treated as equity funds by the taxman, they are eligible for a lower tax rate on capital gains, and might do well for an investor in a high tax bracket. But tax rules can get changed in a moment, as they did for capital gains on debt funds in March 2023, and that must not be the only reason to use a particular category for funds. I would recommend that you keep your debt fund category use small and safe and not try to harvest the highest return.

Equity savings category invests a minimum of 65 per cent in equity, 10 per cent in debt and is allowed arbitrage between spot and futures. They give returns like conservative hybrid funds but because of the favourable tax treatment, might be preferred to those. Remember that any fund with over 65 per cent in equity (or equity-related instruments) will get the equity tax treatment. Therefore, a conservative hybrid is taxed as a debt fund. The tax treatment is good, but the risk metric is marked moderately high on the Risk-o-Meter. You know what I like for my debt portfolio by now! Let's wait till Chapter 9 when we begin to pick categories that we are going to use for our portfolios to decide between the two?

The two solution-oriented categories

Table 4.5

Solution-oriented funds		
	Solution oriented	Scheme characteristics
1	Retirement	Lock-in for a min of five years or retirement age, whichever is earlier
2	Children's	Lock-in for a min of five years or eighteen years of age, whichever is earlier

Table 4.6

Other schemes		
	Others	Scheme characteristics
1	Index/ETFs	Invest a min 95% of assets in index tracked
2	FoF (overseas/ domestic)	Invest a min 95% of assets in underlying fund

These are mainly fund categories that aim to give customized solutions like helping investors plan for retirement and their children's future. You can exit the scheme after a five-year lock-in. Or if you reach retirement age before five years. In the children's fund, if the child reaches age eighteen before the five-year lock-in, then you can exit the fund earlier. The average return in both the categories over time has been similar to equity broad market index returns but with higher expense ratios. The lock-in is useful for people who are unable to take the volatility of the markets and find themselves wanting to exit when markets tank. The lock-in forces them to hold on for the five-year period at least. If you are able to manage your emotions during a down market and stay with an equity index fund, that might be a cheaper option long term which gives similar or better returns.

The two other categories

SEBI has clubbed all the rest of the fund types in this head. So, we have index funds and exchange traded funds (ETFs) as well as other fund types such as overseas and domestic fund of funds.

Index funds and ETFs

Index funds and ETFs have been put under the 'Other Schemes' category. These are very important funds for a fill-it–shut-it–forget-it minded investor and we need to spend time on this category. Get your beverage and prepare to dig in.

To understand an index better, you need to go back and reread the index explanation in *Let's Talk Money* in Chapter 8. Briefly, an index maps the change in the price of a basket of things. These things could be commodities that go into our consumption basket, and the index needed is the consumer price index. Or the things could be stocks, so we get a stock market index. The things could be bonds, and we get a bond price index. In Chapter 8, we will see how such an index is used to reduce our tax liability by inflating the buying price of the past, and thereby reducing the profit offered for tax, typically in a real estate investment.

Index funds and ETFs are called passive funds as against active funds. Active funds are those where the fund manager takes calls of what stocks, bonds or other assets to buy, hold and sell. The fund manager, under the umbrella of the fund category and the investment mandate, must aim to give higher than benchmark index returns to investors. See page 131 in Chapter 6 to understand benchmarks. Active funds have the potential to give investors a much better return experience than simple index returns, though with much higher risk. A passive fund just mimics an index and aims to give investors an easy route to buying all the stocks or bonds in a given index instead of having to buy them separately and maintaining that portfolio.

What's the logic of a passive fund? Most of us are Saravana Bhavan fans. Known for its super-good South Indian food (though it is now repositioned as vegetarian Indian cuisine), the Bhavan experience remains the same across India and across the twenty-two countries it has outlets in. The standard experience every time for a very reasonable cost is the hallmark of the global chain. There are more expensive

South Indian restaurants that might do better food, or might have a specialty that they serve—like Malabar, Chettinad or Andhra cuisine among many others. Now I need to stop and go eat something. Just writing about all these aromatic cuisines is making my mouth water and I'm getting hungry!

What's the relation between investing and these types of cuisines? See, the Bhavan experience is the standard low-cost idli-dosa-pongal-meals experience that most people expect and crave. The more adventurous will try a special cuisine. They will most likely pay more if eating at a fine-dine place. But the overall taste and experience will not be known till the food is eaten. Others before you might have ranked the food, but your experience may differ with the mood of the chef today or the quality of the ingredients sourced now. The owner of the specialty restaurant has a view that people will want something more than the standard fare and will be willing to pay for it. The chef is now entrusted to deliver this experience. Replace the chef with the fund manager and the owner with the asset management company and we have an active fund.

So, an active fund hopes to beat the benchmark and give better returns to the investor for a higher price. See page 111 in Chapter 6 on costs. A passive fund hopes to just give index returns. The two broad market indices in India—S&P BSE Sensex and Nifty 50—are the bellwether indices. The year-on-year return for the past thirty years on these indices has been around 14 per cent. If you just bought all the thirty stocks on the Sensex or the fifty in the Nifty and held them, not changing the stocks unless the composition of the index changed, you would have got the index return, which is not a bad return at all. All that a passive fund does is to give you a product that does the work for you and you do not need to manage the thirty or fifty stocks and their inclusion and exclusion from the index.

Passive funds are great options for investors who are new to mutual funds in general, and are new to equity investing in particular. These are also great products to give your portfolio an exposure to metals like gold and silver. In fact, gold ETF was one of the first ETFs to come to the Indian market. Silver ETFs and index funds are a relatively new fund type as we stand here in 2023. But remember that today, the passive industry is offering very high-risk choices with bespoke indices. For example, in the US, there are passive funds that track an index on crypto currencies or on companies that use blockchain. We do not want to go there. We want to use index investing to reduce the risk of our equity portfolio.

Index funds and ETFs

There are two kinds of passive funds—index funds and ETFs. An index fund is a simple mutual fund that mimics an index and works like all other mutual funds. Now, what is an ETF? Very simply, it is an index fund that is listed on the stock market and is available for trading all day at live prices through the day, unlike a mutual fund that is open for sale and repurchase at the closing price of the day.

Index funds have historically been more expensive than ETFs, but now there are index funds on the Sensex and Nifty 50 that cost as little as 15–20 basis points. Here, 15 basis points means 0.15 per cent and for a fuller understanding of costs of a fund, go to page 111 in Chapter 6. While you can buy and sell an index fund straight to the AMC, you have to open a demat account to trade in an ETF and that might have higher costs, especially if you are going through your bank. Low-cost brokerages have now reduced the cost of trading to very tiny amounts, but it is still something you have to pay. Then there is also the difference between the buying and selling price in an ETF that considers the margin of the market makers who provide liquidity in the ETF market.

The ETFs might also have a problem of liquidity while the mutual fund is obligated to buy at net asset value (NAV)—if there are no loads—any quantity the investor wants to buy or sell. The ETF structure needs a buyer at the other end if you are selling, unlike an index fund. The lack of a buyer might prevent you from selling at the current NAV the quantity you want to sell. The ETFs might also not have the systematic investment plan (SIP) option, and all the other options of entry and exit that we will see in Chapter 5.

The industry is constantly evolving and ETFs started out to give active traders in passive funds a route to trade through the day. Now, active ETFs is a category in the US where a strategy is employed by the fund manager to give a higher return. We are yet to allow such ETFs on the Indian stock market. SEBI does not restrict the number of index funds or

ETFs that a fund house can launch and India is beginning to see new kinds of index funds come to market.

To end the index fund versus ETF debate, my advice is that for an average retail passive investor, it is a good idea to stay with index funds rather than ETFs. You need to find an index fund with a low expense ratio and a low tracking error and we will find out more about this on page 225 in Chapter 11. Traders don't really need an ETF—they have the entire market to trade on.

Fund of funds and overseas funds

A mutual fund that invests in a bunch of other mutual funds is called a fund of funds. The idea is to get the diversification of a number of different funds into just one product. India had a very early experiment with this concept when ING Investment Management promoted a multi-manager fund house called Optimix AMC in 2006. This was going to be a no-bias fund of funds offering with the idea to create a product that would invest in such schemes of all fund houses which would give an investor the best possible option without having to go to different funds. The concept was ahead of its time and the fund house folded up in the next two years.

Fund of funds today invest in same fund house schemes. Not very popular due to the debt fund taxation rules even on equity funds, these fund types have been used by fund houses to offer life-cycle funds and overseas funds. Go to page 176 in Chapter 8 to understand the FoF taxation. These are also being used to offer ETFs to passive fund investors who do not want to go the ETF route—for example, Bharat Bond Fund of Funds only invests in Bharat Bond ETF.

The overseas fund of funds are a great option for those wanting geographical diversification in overseas stocks without having to deal with brokerages and the clunky process of investing aboard. The overseas funds are ranked so high on risk that they are off the Risk-o-Meter and have been given a risk grade of seven, while the Risk-o-Meter ends at risk level six!

Fund of funds pay the expenses of the underlying fund and are allowed to charge investors an expense ratio as well. Though there are SEBI limits on what these can charge (page 118, Chapter 6) investors need to check out the combined expense ratio before investing.

I know it is exhausting to read about all the categories. There is really too much choice, isn't there? As we get to the chapter on choosing funds, I will find a way of cutting down the categories we need to engage with before we start choosing actual schemes. Again, remember that it is important to choose categories before you choose schemes. We want to match your investment objectives to the right category before we get to fund selection. Like we need to choose the car category—hatchback, sedan, SUV or luxury—before we get down to actual brand and specification choice.

So, the TV was bought. I reduced the choice set by fixing the size that would work for the room, the picture and sound quality and by defining a budget within which I would place my final choice. Now I just had to choose from three options and making the choice was a breeze. The FIFA on the new TV is exhilarating and much better than trying to watch the match split screen as the TV warmed up earlier!

We try to buy mutual funds by looking at the schemes directly without first understanding our needs and matching some of the thirty-seven categories to them. SEBI has made huge progress in putting up the rules of the game so that an average investor is able to get what they need when they choose through a category selection first.

You are doing okay if you understand that

1. though there are thirty-seven categories, you don't need them all;
2. equity and debt have different attributes and you need a mix of them;
3. you can choose categories to meet your short-, medium- and long-term needs;
4. choosing a category first is much easier than looking at thousands of options;
5. active funds expose you to fund-manager risk; and
6. index funds are the least cost way to get broad market index returns.

5

ENTRY AND EXIT OPTIONS

Not just the entry but the exit door must be examined before you commit to travel or an investment.

Think of a room, let's call it trapped-you room, where a movie is playing. You can enter for a price, but once you enter, you are forced to sit for the entire three hours. No bathroom break. No cell phone break. If you really want to get out, you need to pay half the ticket fee. At the end of three hours, you can get out for free. If you did not like the movie, you have no option but to sit it out, or pay up to get out. The movie might turn out to be super good and you might have memories for a lifetime after watching it. Still, would you enter this room?

There is another room, let's call it your-choice room, in the same building, where there is no cost of entry, no cost of exit, but you need to pay a small fee to stay seated for the three hours every one hour. You can exit anytime you want. If you like the movie, after an hour you can pay and continue to sit. If you don't, you can get out and not pay for the entire movie. Do you like this option?

The trapped-you room is a standard endowment or money-back policy that insurance companies sell. The your-choice room is the most common type of mutual fund where there are no restrictions on entry and exit.

Entry and exit options are very important in a long-term financial product and go beyond the simplistic example I have just described. You have to choose amongst many options on entry and a wrong choice will impact the future of your money. The final choice of an investment product must consider the cost, efficiency and lock-ins. As I will repeat a million times at the risk of irritating you—a good investment is not just one that gives the highest return!

We will first work through three kinds of mutual funds on offer—open-ended, close-ended and hybrid of open and close. Next, we will understand the various options in a mutual fund that you need to choose on entry and exit.

Open, close and hybrid

Open-ended funds are always open for sale and repurchase. They don't have an end date. When you invest in a five-year FD, the investment tenor is five years. It is fifteen years in a PPF. It is twenty years usually in an insurance endowment product. Open-ended funds are forever funds that never shut down unless the fund house winds them down due to a variety of reasons such as lack of investor interest. Or, due to regulatory changes, the fund is merged with another or shut down fully. This means that the fund house can create an unlimited number of units over the lifetime of the scheme as more and more investors buy into that scheme. No, the value of the fund does not fall as more units are created—this is not a stock, but a unit that has little bits of shares and bonds of forty to seventy companies. You will understand this better when you read about the NAV on page 124 in Chapter 6. The assets under management of these funds can go on rising as more investors buy the fund, but they are divided into the bundles of stocks and bonds they invest in.

The oldest open-ended scheme in India is the UTI Mastershare that launched on 18 October 1986. The annual return since launch as on 6 April 2023 is 16.99 per cent. To get this return, the investor needed to simply hold the scheme through all of the market ups and downs over thirty-six and some years of its existence.

One of the earliest private company schemes, Franklin India Bluechip Fund launched on 1 December 1993 and its return since inception is an annual 18.93 per cent as on 6 April 2023. Rs 1 lakh invested on that date is worth Rs 1.5 crore. Breathtaking returns, but this is not a sales pitch for these two funds. This is just an indication of the length of time that has elapsed since their launch and how these schemes are still open for investment. Since then, many new funds are in the market and we will get to how to choose schemes for your portfolio soon. It is a long walk, but we will get there.

Close-ended funds are those that have a subscription window after which you can only redeem your units at the date on which the scheme ends. These work like FDs or endowment plans without the guarantees, of course. The number of units remains the same over the lifetime of the fund. To give liquidity to investors, the rules make listing of close-ended schemes on a stock exchange mandatory. This means that investors don't sell units to the fund house (the way they do in an open-ended scheme) but can sell to other investors on the stock market like you do in direct shares. At the close date of the scheme, investors redeem their units to the fund house and get their money back.

Many errors were made in the initial years of the mutual fund industry with this category of funds. After UTI, only public sector firms were allowed initially into the mutual fund business and most of the sponsors were banks. They were afraid to launch open-ended schemes and preferred to do the close-ended version. And because they were used to guarantees in bank deposits, some of the bank-promoted funds gave guarantees in a market-linked product like a mutual fund. In a famous case, investors, who were promised a guaranteed return by Canara Bank–sponsored Canstar fund, went to court when the fund house reneged on its promise. And won! In a rare case of retail investor victory, the fund house was forced to honour its guaranteed return commitment. Such products phased out very quickly once the true nature of a market-linked product was understood both by investors and the industry.

Close-ended funds have also been used by the industry cynically to harvest higher fees during 2006 to 2008 when the new fund offer charges were removed for open-ended funds but close-ended funds were allowed to charge the huge 6 per cent (of the amount collected during the NFO). Fund houses quickly switched to launching close-ended funds and one academic paper found that investors lost more than US$ 500 million in extra fees during this twenty-two month period before these fees were banned for close-ended funds as well.[1]

Close-ended funds got a new lease of life with the fixed maturity plan (FMP) product that mimicked a fixed deposit—a close-ended debt fund with a maturity period between one and five years, but with only an indicative return rather than a fixed guaranteed return. The FMPs buy bonds that mature just before the date of redemption for the investor. A bond fund has two major sources of risk—interest rate risk and credit risk—which we will read about in detail in Chapter 7. The FMPs took care of the interest rate risk as they bought bonds that had the same maturity period as the tenor of the FMP. In good quality bonds, there is very little interest rate risk if these bonds are held to maturity. The risk comes if you sell midway in the secondary market. Being close-ended for sale and repurchase—FMPs did away with investors exiting midway and making a loss.

But the financial sector will never let a good idea stay good for too long. So, slowly the one-year FMPs became two- and three- and then five-year FMPs. The distributor commission got higher and higher as the five-year commissions were upfronted and given to the distributor. Then, in a bid to show higher and higher returns, some fund houses began to lower the credit quality. We know that the higher the riskiness of a bond, the lower the credit rating and the higher the interest rate the bond will have to offer to attract investors. Government bonds are called gilt-edged because the risk of default is zero. A few instances of FMPs not paying back investors on the date of redemption caused the cracks in the FMP market to show up. The interest rate risk was taken care of, but the credit risk came back to bite investors who wanted the higher return, but did not understand the higher risk attached.

No wonder that from 25 per cent of the debt fund AUM in March 2014, FMPs dropped to 10 per cent in March 2018 and then just 3 per cent in March 2022. From being sold as a higher return FD, FMPs became a bad word after 2020 when many schemes saw a rollover at the due date and a drop in the indicated return.

A problem with the FMPs was also the rigid structure of the product where there was no option to redeem with the fund house during the tenor of the product. Liquidity-seeking investors needed to go to the secondary market to get a much lower price than what the NAV was indicating.

Hybrid between open ended and close ended

The industry innovated to bring to market a hybrid between an open-ended and a close-ended product and this was called an interval fund. It invests both in debt and equity, though it stays mostly in the debt space. This fund opens and shuts at periodic intervals and investors have an opportunity to exit.

A new version of an interval fund is the target maturity fund (TMF) that is an open-ended passive debt fund with a stated maturity date. Open ended means that the fund is open for sales and repurchase at all times and does not tie the investor into a particular date. A passive fund means that it tracks an index. This index could be an existing one or the fund can get an index constructed and track it. With the active bond picking removed, the fund-manager risk is reduced. The maturity date is when the bonds in the portfolio will mature giving the indicated return as shown by the yield of the portfolio. The TMFs have a date in their names. This is the date on which the bond portfolio it holds will mature. Investors who want to redeem can do so, or they can hold and the fund will buy another basket of bonds and rename the same TMF according to the new maturity date. For example, the SBI CPSE Bond Plus SDL Sep 2026 50:50 index fund will mature in September 2026. It tracks an index of bonds of central public sector enterprises and state development loans. On its own, a state-development loan might be very risky, but when several are bundled along with the CPSEs, the overall risk reduces. This does sound very jargonish. It is enough to know that both interest rate and fund-manager risk is low in this fund type and the credit risk can be understood from the nature of the index the fund tracks. A corporate bond index will have a higher risk than a government bond index. Since, TMFs today are allowed to only invest in government securities, PSU bonds and SDLs, they are relatively lower risk than a fund with corporate bonds. Also, debt-fund investors can look at the Risk-o-Meter to see if the risk is indeed low or not.

Of the two advantages of this hybrid fund, one got removed on 1 April 2023. This was the lower tax and indexation benefit if held for three years. Read about the tax treatment of debt funds on page 176 in Chapter 8. The other advantage stays of it being a passive fund, which ensures that the expense ratio will remain under 1 per cent according to SEBI rules. In the FMP road rage, some fund houses were padding up the expense ratios to over 2 per cent for a debt fund, which took a toll on the returns to investors.

In terms of choice, you are mostly going to stay with open-ended funds, both in equity and in debt. Ideally, we want the doors for entry and exit to be open at all times. Only in special circumstances do we get into a product that has a lock on the exit door, for example, in PPF or our PF or even an ELSS. But you should know what is out there. Also, the innovation pace in the industry is swift and more product types will certainly arrive. It helps you to know the basics so that you can evaluate whatever it is that the market throws at you.

Direct and regular

You might have seen the words direct and regular in the names of the schemes you were browsing through. A regular plan is one that is sold by an intermediary like a distributor, a bank or even a platform. A direct plan is one that is bought directly from the fund house. The difference between the two is the reduction in the cost of distribution—the agent commission. A direct plan is cheaper by the amount of the trail commission paid in the regular plan to the intermediary. (Skip ahead to page 118 in Chapter 6 for trail commissions.) It is like going to the factory outlet rather than a shop in the mall for the same branded pair of shoes—the factory outlet is cheaper because it removes the cost of distribution.

A bit of history here first to understand the 'why' of this better. Till the year 2012, mutual funds used to offer two kinds of plans on the same portfolio—retail and institutional. The retail scheme had a lower entry threshold of investment and institutional money needed to be Rs 1 crore. The expense ratio of the retail option was double that of the institutional option. Retail was, in a way, subsidizing the larger money that had greater bargaining power with the mutual funds. In 2012, SEBI removed this distinction but introduced a new variant—the direct and regular plans. They would have the same portfolio, but the expense ratio of the direct plan will be lower to the extent of the trail commission that would be added in a regular plan. By 2012, the front commissions were gone and AMCs were paying for distribution out of their expense ratios.

Costs matter in financial products. We will read much more about costs in Chapter 6, but what you need to know is that a 1 percentage point difference in the cost over thirty years means a difference of about 30 per cent to your money.

You invest Rs 5 lakh in both direct and regular plans of the same mutual fund scheme that grows at 7 per cent in the regular plan and 8 per cent in the direct plan (the 1 percentage point is the cost difference, and since they have the same portfolio, the returns are the same, just the cost is different). Thirty years later, the regular plan is now worth Rs 38 lakh and the direct plan is worth Rs 50 lakh. You are Rs 12 lakh richer in the direct plan.

So, you should always only invest in the direct plan, right? Wrong.

Like I said, the highest return might not be the best route for you. This will differ from person to person. A good distributor will give many services starting from portfolio construction (a very complicated exercise for most people), maintaining the portfolio, updating you on changes in funds, managing the contact detail changes, the nominations, the tax work, the rebalancing and many other maintenance jobs that an active portfolio needs. For some super busy people or someone with no knowledge about funds, to go with a regular plan might be a better option than to struggle on your own using the direct option. Investing is not a one-time job, but an active portfolio needs to be looked after on a regular basis. The one situation in which a direct approach is always better is if you are only investing in a broad market index fund with a fill-it–shut-it–forget-it mindset. Then it makes no sense to pay commission to a seller. Or if the bank is doing nothing much in terms of all the services I had listed out, you are better off going direct. But there are distributors I know who add so much value that the higher expense ratio is fully worth it.

There is another option now that many high net worth investors are going for—they use the advisory services of a registered investment advisor (RIA) and then use his services to buy only the direct plan. They compensate the advisor through an annual fee. This is still a nascent market and you might find it difficult to find an RIA easily since there are few of them.

You can access the direct plan from the mutual fund office itself or their website. But soon you will see that this is a clunky process. A portfolio needs at least six to ten schemes and to go to each fund house is a pain. There are now platforms that allow you to transact either for a small fee or free of cost. Mutual Fund Utility (mfuonline.com) is one such platform that has been set up by the industry itself. There are others like execution-only platforms that are stock brokers but allow mutual fund investors to onboard direct plans for no fees right now. An RIA will also offer the direct plan. The regular option is available through individual agents,[2] banks, corporate agents and platforms that curate your portfolio for you.

Growth and dividend

A question I have to answer many times is this: should I now get out of my mutual funds? I find myself grasping around for an answer. I don't even know where to begin, the problem with this question is so fundamental. When you invest in mutual funds, it is not a tactical short-term punt. You are using this route for the various solutions you need over your lifetime. These are short-term, medium-term and long-term solutions. The trading mindset has to be set aside when you invest through mutual funds. If it is trading you want to do, there is the day trading and futures markets for you—these are regulated parts of the market and are great for those who want to spend a part of their day trading. But do remember that nine of ten investors lose money on futures and options in India. But if you are investing, then the texture of your questions needs to change. There is no 'good' time to get in and out of mutual funds. There are some equity funds that are lifetime funds—you simply never get out of them and bequeath them to your kids, just as you would that two-BHK in Andheri. The mutual fund bequeath, in fact, would be far easier and kids won't be able to litigate on it if the nominations are in place. And ... let's leave this for another book? The inheritance story is long, heartbreaking and needs far more attention than I intend to give just yet.

Your reason for investing in a fund will determine the next set of choices you are faced with when you set out to buy a mutual fund—whether you want to periodically milk the portfolio, target a certain amount in the future, or just let the tree become an orchard. You have to choose between a growth plan and an income distribution with capital withdrawal plan or IDCW (called dividend plan earlier).

A growth plan allows the money invested to keep growing. The number of units remains the same (unless you buy more units, of course), but the net asset value (NAV) keeps growing over time in a well-performing fund. Read about NAV on page 124, Chapter 6. The NAV grows as the stocks and bonds bought by the mutual fund grow in value. If you do not redeem any units, then the value of your investment continues to grow over time because the number of units multiplied by NAV is the value of your investment, which grows as the NAV rises. For example, if you bought 10,000 units of a scheme at NAV of Rs 50, your invested amount is Rs 5 lakh and if the NAV grows to Rs 100, your money grows to Rs 10 lakh (Rs 100 × 10,000 units).

Of course, the value can fall if the fund manager is not good or if there is a downturn in the markets as a whole. But over time, in a growing economy, well-chosen funds do well and grow your money.

The income distribution and capital withdrawal (IDCW) option allows you to receive a mix of interest, dividend and profit at intervals that the mutual fund fixes. Quickly recall here that savings become investments when they are put in debt, equity and real assets. These assets can throw off *income* in the form of interest, dividend and rent. The assets also throw off *profit* which is called capital gain. This terminology is important, as we will see in Chapter 8 on taxation. In an IDCW option, the mutual fund will periodically dip into the gains and hand it out to you.

Imagine this very simplistic way of understanding the difference between the growth and IDCW options: there is a portfolio whose NAV, which is Rs 100, grows by Rs 20. The investor in the growth plan sees her NAV rise to Rs 120. For the investor in the IDCW plan, the mutual fund hands out Rs 20 of profit and the NAV stays at Rs 100. The number of units in both options remains the same. The portfolio remains the same.

You might say that when you look at the NAVs of one of India's oldest funds—Franklin India Bluechip Fund—the growth NAV is at Rs 680.7679 and the IDCW NAV is at Rs 37.7250 (as on 6 April 2023), why is the distribution option NAV not at Rs 10 (which is the original NAV at scheme launch)? What happens is that fund houses don't release all of the gains on the portfolio to investors; they release a part of it. In the above example, instead of releasing Rs 20 in the distribution option, the fund will release only Rs 15. Rs 5 stays in the portfolio (as it does in the growth scheme), taking the NAV to Rs 105. In the case of the Franklin fund, Rs 5 lakh invested at Rs 10 NAV is now at Rs 3.4 crore in the growth option, but is worth Rs 18.9 lakh. Rs 3.2 crore has been distributed out to this investor over the lifetime of this fund as dividend or distributed income! Why do funds not distribute all of the gain? I would imagine, to keep the capital ahead of inflation would be just one easy explanation.

The clumsy-sounding IDCW name change from the earlier dividend option happened on 1 April 2021. We will need to dive back into regulatory history to see why this happened. The word dividend is understood by investors as something that is a sharing of profit, which is not due to a sale of the shares that reduces the capital holding of the investor. As we will see in example after example in the mutual fund industry, some rogue fund houses take a good idea and stretch it to the edge of regulatory limits and then finally go over. SEBI had to change the name 'dividend' as some fund houses began selling the option as a guaranteed return of 1 per cent a month (more than 12 per cent a year) return product. Nothing was said in writing, but the bank branches (usually the sponsor bank) and agents were verbally assuring this return. Some bank-promoted AMCs were at the forefront of this investor cheating. But mutual funds invest in market securities whose value goes up and down. For the months that there was no 'profit' to distribute, the mutual funds were dipping into the investors' capital and redeeming units to pay out the 'dividend'. Regular income-seeking investors are usually the retired and this action of the fund houses doing this fraud was deeply harmful to senior citizens. SEBI finally took note and did two things. One, changed the name from the misleading dividend to IDCW. Two, ensured that MFs made the disclosure that under this option a certain portion of investor's capital can be distributed as dividend.

When we see the ever-tightening noose of regulation on the mutual fund industry, there is a sense of regulatory overreach or complaints of micro-regulation. But honestly, having been a member of SEBI's Mutual Fund Committee for over a decade, all I can say is that unless SEBI does this, the industry will find ways to hoodwink investors. The mutual fund industry had done well overall, but a few sharp practices of some fund houses encourages a race to the bottom with many other AMCs doing similar things. Therefore, the regulator has to step in to prevent small investors who do not understand the complexity of getting cheated.

Three kinds of IDCW

There are three options to choose from on the income-distribution road. Overall, this set of options is not a good idea because of the tax disadvantage that dividends have over a short- or long-term capital gain route. (Read page 178 in Chapter 8.) Tax rules can change but we must still learn about them so that we are not taken by surprise when faced with the IDCW choices at the point of buying the funds.

A variant of the IDCW is the reinvestment option. This was the dividend reinvestment option earlier. When the mutual fund industry was set up, concepts like mark-to-market and daily NAV were alien. The risk-averse investors chose the FD-plus-life insurance route and some people bought direct stocks, and were familiar with the concept of dividends. The dividend-reinvestment option simply put back the distributed gains into the same portfolio by buying more units. In the earlier example, if Rs 15 was distributed, then that money was used to buy fresh units at the current NAV. The net result was the same as in the growth option in terms of the final value of the investment. In this case the NAV went down (Rs 105), but the number of units increased. The number of units would equal the current NAV divided by the amount reinvested, that is, Rs 105 divided by Rs 15 or 0.1429 units. Unless there is some taxation advantage in the future, stay away from this option as well.

The third variant is the transfer option of the IDCW. The gain handed out under the IDCW option is parked in another fund so that the investor can use it at a later date. The logic of this option is like this: suppose you have a defined need of money in two years and you want to park some of the profits from your equity funds over these two years towards a part of that goal. Then you might choose the transfer option of the IDCW and ask the fund to park the money in an ultra-short-term debt fund or a money market fund. If you forgot what these are, go back to page 58 in Chapter 4 and just take another look. We need to get used to these fund categories since we will make great use of them over our entire investing journey. The idea is good, but the route is not, because of the way dividends are taxed at present. They get added to your slab rate and those in the 20 per cent, 30 per cent and higher brackets end up paying a higher tax on dividends than they would on short- and long-term capital gains in equity funds. There is another option to take home your regular income and profits, and transfer the money for a more liquid product—which we will meet soon—called a systematic withdrawal plan. We will read about this in Chapter 8 on taxation. The IDCW option has yet more choice in the form of daily, weekly, fortnightly and monthly payouts.

Which do you pick of the four routes? Pick the growth option. Only in cases where you are at a 10 per cent tax rate on income tax does the IDCW option become a better choice than growth under the current tax regime.

Lump sum, SIP, STP

I was on a flight one general election result day and by the time the passengers switched on their phones, it looked as if India was going to have a new set of faces in the government.

The guy sitting ahead of me whipped out his phone and barked out an order for some shares. From his body language it seemed that he was going to make a major market-moving investment. I could not help but overhear the loud talk coming from ahead of me—the order was for some 500 shares of a blue-chip stock. The guy was behaving like the big bull of Dalal Street, but his order was not even a decimal point in the total number of shares of the company he was buying in.

The point of this story is that one of the big bhoots in the investing world is the ghost of the big hitter, the smashing winner of the stock markets, the big bull. The bhoot haunts the average retail investor making them believe that they are going to make a 'killing' on the market. That they will either carry out that fortune-making sale or purchase and then live happily ever after. Real life is not like this. Most of us have regular flows of income and spends. We save on a regular basis as well. Even people with irregular flows of income will manage to make investments several times a year rather than one big lump sum at the end of the financial year. This flow of money is not a one-time stream. It will continue over your entire earning, spending, saving and investing lifetime and then in the milking of the corpus post retirement. These decisions are there till the last moment of your life—so let go of this one-time-big-hit mindset. Crash diets do not work. Crash workouts do not work. Crash investing just loses you money and peace of mind.

There are two routes to investing—making a large lump-sum investment or making regular investments over the year. A third looks to convert the lump sum into a staggered investment over a period of time. Each have their place in your world. Let's get to know them better.

Lump-sum investing is when you go to the market one day and invest a large chunk of money. Typically, this has been the tax-saving investing habit for most middle-class Indians for decades. Over the months of January, February and March, people rush to complete the Section 80C investments to get the benefit of the deduction that will lower their tax burden. Most people make a one-time investment during that time of the year and have got into the habit of doing all their investments during this time as well. When you are doing a long-term-guaranteed return investment as in a PPF, it does not make any difference on the risk side—the value of the PPF investment will not suddenly fall; it is a guaranteed return from the central government. But should you do the same in an equity fund and the market suddenly crashes, you will lose a chunk of your capital. Lump-sum investments are not a good idea when investing in a short-term-volatile instrument such as equity. Certain categories of debt funds are far less volatile and lump-sum investments can be made in this part of the market.

So, what is a good way? Going via the SIP route. An SIP is like a recurring deposit where a certain pre-decided amount of money goes into a selected scheme or set of schemes. The logic is simple—match the saving rhythm of a person with an investing option. At one level, an SIP allows the regular savings of a person to get converted to a regular investment without having to decide each month what to do with the fresh savings. There is another financial logic to an SIP and it is called rupee cost averaging. This just means that when you put a fixed amount in a mutual fund, you tend to buy more when markets are down and buy less when markets are up.

Imagine that you are investing Rs 50,000 a month in an index fund that has an NAV of Rs 100 on 4 January 2020. You get 500 units. On 5 February, the NAV rises to 105 and you buy 476 units (I am ignoring the decimals). By 5 April, the pandemic panic has set in and the NAV has fallen to Rs 85. This month your Rs 50,000 is buying you 588 units. By December 2020, the NAV is up to Rs 120 and your unit purchase number is 417. Notice how you are buying fewer units when the price is high and more units when the price is low?

To go contrary to market movements is psychologically very difficult. Most retail investors in the world tend to sell equity when markets fall and buy when they are at lifetime highs. The SIP route builds in basic investing hygiene in its very structure so that you, the investor, will not get afraid to take a decision to invest in the middle of a crash. Your decision was taken long ago and your SIP deduction happens from the bank automatically. You can stop your SIP of course, but most people in India tend to continue them as they have seen the benefits of SIP investing over the years. No wonder that the SIP flow into mutual funds is growing each year. The SIP, it seems, was introduced in India by Franklin Templeton AMC in 1993 but it took more than a decade for the concept to be tried and tested before being adopted by the Indian investor. What began as a trickle in 1993 grew to just under Rs 4,000 crore a month in 2016–17, and is now at over Rs 13,500 crore a month in 2022–23. More than Rs 1.3 trillion a year is flowing into the Indian markets through this route. This is pure retail money that is investing in a risk-bearing product. In conferences on retail finance across the world, the Indian SIP success story is being discussed! The value-seeking Indian consumer has become a sensible equity investor through the SIP route.

There are other advantages of an SIP. It makes investing a habit. It removes savings from spending at the beginning of the month. You can choose the date of the SIP, but most people end up choosing the first seven days of the month so that the money is saved and invested before it can get spent.

There is yet another unintended consequence of the SIP success story. Till twenty years ago, the Indian stock market was driven by the fat pipelines of foreign institutional and portfolio investors, or foreign investors who invested in the Indian stock markets. Each time the foreign portfolio investments (FPIs) would exit the Indian markets, they would crash. The joke was that when Wall Street sneezes, India catches a cold. But how that has changed in the past twenty years! The availability of domestic retail money that comes consistently each month has delinked us from the mood swings of global hot money. India is no longer at the mercy of some large speculator who can cause a crash in our markets anymore. The credit goes to each of us who uses this route to invest sensibly on our growth story as we rise from being the world's fifth largest economy to the third largest in the next decade.

There are many misconceptions about SIPs. First, that it is a product by itself. 'I am investing in SIPs' is like saying 'I am eating atta'. Atta is the raw material that goes into making roti, parantha, poori, kulcha (especially when you have it with chanas, it is amazing!). But then mirchi parantha.... We really need to get back to SIPs!

An SIP is a *route* and not the destination. When you say you are travelling, you don't just say I am taking a flight, you say, I am taking a flight to Chennai. The destination of the flight is Chennai. Each SIP has a destination fund. You are investing in that through the route of an SIP. It can be any scheme across equity, debt, gold and combinations of these. The correct way to think about this is: I am investing through an SIP into GrowSteady Equity Fund of Good Result Mutual Fund. SIP is a route.

Next, SIPs can lead you to any kind of a mutual fund scheme and not just an equity scheme, though they're the most popular destination of SIPs. You can use an SIP to invest even in a debt or a gold scheme or a multi-asset scheme.

For a seamless SIP setup, you need to either have a distributor who collects post-dated cheques for the twelve or twenty-four or more SIPs you plan to do. Most people prefer to link their bank accounts to a platform and then make a digital mandate for the SIP amount, date and duration of investment. We will read more about setting up an easy flow process in Chapter 13.

Some fund houses limit the SIP amount you can invest each month. Mirae Asset Emerging Bluechip Fund (as in April 2023) has limited the monthly SIP to just Rs 2,500 per PAN number. SBI Mutual fund has restricted inflows into its small-cap fund to Rs 25,000 a month. These fund houses do not want more money than they can deploy into the market and therefore restrict the inflows. This makes them actually even more sought-after!

SIP options

The industry has innovated very hard in the SIP space and you have a whole list of options available to set up your SIP. You need to decide how much of a monthly commitment you want to make and in how many schemes. We will be choosing schemes in Chapter 10, so come back here and read this again when you begin the SIP-creation process.

Next, you need to decide the date of the SIP debit from your bank account. If you have created the three-account system you read in *Let's Talk Money*, this debit will be from your Invest-It account. What? Not read it abhi tak? Abhi ke abhi go and read! Some fund houses allow you to choose your own dates for the SIP and some fund houses give you options across four or five dates that you can choose from. Both work just fine.

You can sign up for the time period that you want to invest for—a year, two years, five. Or some investors who have used this route for the past few years sign up for a 'perpetual' SIP. That means the SIP continues till the time you put a stop to it. Investors have gained knowledge and confidence over the past investing years and are happier to let the SIP run unless they want to stop it. And then it takes at most one SIP cycle to get out of it.

The plain, vanilla SIP sees one outflow on a certain date of the month. It could be Rs 15,000 each in three equity schemes on the fourth of every month. You can choose between various options—daily SIP, weekly, fortnightly, monthly or quarterly SIP. Most people prefer a monthly SIP as it matches their income flows. There is very little to be gained by trying to do a daily or weekly SIP. Over a thirty-year period of investing, the difference in a daily and monthly SIP will disappear.

Investor needs can vary. So, there are flexible SIPs, where you can increase or decrease the amount you want to invest each month. This is particularly useful for people with irregular income flows like consultants and gig workers.

See if the fund you finally choose and the platform through which you are investing allows for this facility.

Some funds allow you to skip an instalment if you inform the fund house a week before the SIP due date. This is useful when a sudden emergency strikes and you have not built up your emergency fund enough or even that is not enough and you need to pause your SIP for a few months.

Another option is the top-up SIP that allows you to increase the money you are investing by a fixed amount or percentage every year. You can give a mandate to increase your SIP each year by say, 10 per cent or Rs 5,000 (usually in multiples of Rs 500) every year. This automatically ensures a rising savings and investment amount that soaks up the annual rise in salary that most people see. But these are usually rigid products and cannot be changed once they are set in motion.

While all the options described are very attractive, keeping it simple is useful. Some of these options will not allow an exit and you will have to stop the SIP, for example, in the top-up plan. Start a simple monthly SIP; you can always stop it and start another one of a higher or lower amount through your platform in the same scheme.

STP

There is one elderly uncle who is FD-loving and stock market-hating on most days. But when the Sensex and Nifty 50 go on an upward rampage and hit lifetime highs, he gets an itch that he needs to scratch. He begins to incessantly message, call and get others in the family to call me asking for a recommendation to buy a mutual fund. *Koi naam batao, kisme dalen abhi saat lakh?* Where do I put my Rs 7 lakh, tell me a name now! Over the years, I have learnt not to respond to these panic-laden FOMO calls. He has burnt his fingers many times in the past twenty years because markets periodically make lifetime highs—from 5,000 Sensex to 15,000, then 25,000 and now all the way up above 60,000—and he tends to throw a bucket of money at the market. This money quickly falls in value because the stock market is long term steady upwards, but short term very up and down. A lifetime high is usually followed by a period of sideways movement or even a crash sometimes. At market crash, he exits and swears never to enter again, blaming the person who gave him the market tip on which stock or fund to buy—grumbling about the government, the PM, his prodigal son ... basically everybody in the world! Till the next lifetime high. Uncle has failed to understand that it is not the quality of advice but his desire to hit the market with a large sum of money, especially if he does not have the staying power of reason and conviction in the market.

For people like uncle particularly, and the rest of us generally, it is not a good idea to put a large sum of money into the stock market on one day. Nobody can predict the short-term journey of a stock market, and a global event like a war, a pandemic or a financial crisis might take the market down by a large chunk over a very short period of time. It is very scary to see your Rs 7 lakh dissolve into nothing, and be left with Rs 4 or 5 lakh in just a few months. Of course, the money will recover if the fund choice is good, as markets eventually recover, but the mental agony of losing money can be managed by turning the lump sum into an SIP.

This is done by using a systematic transfer plan (STP) that collects the lump sum in a low-risk debt scheme and at periodic intervals (decided by you) funds an equity scheme. If uncle had invested that Rs 7 lakh in end-March 2020, by May this money would have been worth Rs 5 lakh. He sold off in disgust and took home Rs 2 lakh of loss. Had he held on till the end of the year, he would have recovered the money and ended the twelve-month period up by Rs 50,000. But had he staggered the investment into Rs 58,000 a month over twelve months, he would have been sitting on Rs 8.3 lakh at the end of the year.

You can use this facility by first choosing the equity fund you want to invest in and then from the *same* fund house, choose a liquid fund to park your lump sum in. Remember to choose a growth option, with low expense ratio with no exit load. Then set up the transfer choosing the amount you want to invest every month from the liquid to the equity. When I set up my first STP many years back, I make a rookie error of choosing a liquid fund of one fund house but an equity fund of another! The same fund house will allow a switch from one scheme to another and this facility is not there between two different fund houses (it should be, but that is another policy debate).

You can also keep the money in a bank and create an SIP. There are two reasons to choose an STP over keeping the large lump sum in the bank. One, large dumps of money end up being spent, lent or put in emotion-driven impulse investments. The money is out of reach of a debit card or a digital payment app when it sits in a liquid fund. Two, a liquid fund is better than an FD on flexibility and ease of operation.

With how much can you begin an STP? The industry norm is a minimum corpus of Rs 12,000 that makes for twelve Rs 1,000 STP or six Rs 2,000 transactions. There is no upper limit on how much you can move and over what period of time between two schemes of the same fund house. Most investors use this facility to park their bonus money, large refunds, loans paid back by family or friends, profits from some investment liquidated like the sale of some property or inherited money.

You can use the STP to move from equity to debt as well, though this is less used than the reverse. You can book profits from an equity fund if either you are rebalancing or have a goal approaching and you want to start milking the equity fund. These can be transferred into a low-risk liquid or a money market fund (choose the debt fund depending on when you need the money; see Chapter 10 on how to choose schemes). Again, you need to be careful to set this up between the schemes of the same fund house.

There are options even on the STP route. Of course, the mutual fund industry will not leave a thing alone! It is just that the choice set can get so complicated that either people will freeze or will make uninformed choices. I am hoping to help with at least marking out all the choices and then identifying the one most appropriate for you.

One option is a flexible or trigger STP. This can work either from debt to equity or equity to debt. You can specify either a target level of the index or NAV or whatever option your fund house allows to either move money into or out of an equity fund. Suppose you want to invest more each time the market drops by 0.25 percentage points. You can create a pool in a liquid fund and give the mandate to switch Rs 50,000 (for example) each time the NAV drops by 0.25 percentage points. Or, each time the market rises by 1 April, switch Rs 25,000 (or whatever you choose subject to the fund house allowing that amount) from the equity to the liquid scheme of the same fund house.

Remember that every switch will have a tax impact as you move from liquid to equity or vice versa. You need to read Chapter 8 carefully to understand how to get your tax reports at the end of the year when you file your tax returns. A good distributor or advisor will do this work for you.

There are other options in a constantly evolving industry, but it helps to keep the choices simple, especially if you are new to mutual funds and market-linked investing.

Exit options

Whenever I enter a new place—could be an underground parking or a cinema hall—I look for the exit sign immediately.

I need to know from where I can get out of this place. Exits are important—both in contracts, in your workplace and in personal relationships. Anything that is binding blindly has the potential to become toxic. Or dangerous—like cults. That is why I dislike the endowment and money-back plans of life insurance companies. They have very expensive exit costs that eat into the capital. Worse, they are never disclosed upfront on entry.

Your exit from a mutual fund is quite easy both in terms of cost and time taken. The SEBI rules gave mutual funds ten days to return your money on all the schemes, but in real life, the money comes back much faster. Liquid funds usually take just one working day to get your money back in your bank account. Other debt and equity funds take between three or four working days to get your money into your account. If you are working with a distributor, then the redemption request is processed through her; else you can do it yourself through your bank, digital platform or mobile app depending on who you are using to transact.

There are two routes to exit—one is to redeem a lump sum and the second is to set up a systematic withdrawal plan (SWP). A lump sum withdrawal can be based on the number of units you want to redeem, but most people choose a money amount they want to redeem. For example, you might have parked Rs 2 lakh in a liquid fund to pay your contractor for home repair work. When the payment date is near, you will simply put in a redemption request for either all units (if that is all there is in that fund) or Rs 2 lakh. Similarly, in an equity fund, you might want to redeem Rs 5 lakh from a portfolio of Rs 50 lakh you hold in that particular scheme. You will just choose the 'specific amount' option rather than the 'unit number' option.

A very useful option is the SWP that allows you to set up a regular withdrawal amount. Typically used by the retired for their regular income needs, an SWP will redeem units to make available the money on a date chosen by you. I have several super-seniors in the extended family who use this facility really well. The money is in the account at the beginning of the month without them having to make a call or trigger a redemption. They have specified how much money each needs at the top of the month. The only thing the planner or advisor or you as a do-it-yourself investor needs to be careful about is that the rate of withdrawal should not be larger than the rate of growth of the fund. The SWP sees redemption of units, so over a long enough period of time, the units can go down to zero if the withdrawal rate is higher than the growth of the NAV.

If the corpus continues to grow at the expected rate, the number of units redeemed will keep falling, but an unexpected market downturn can throw this strategy off course. Retired people who are fully dependent on this must get good advice to set up such an SWP. Ideally use this as one of the regular income sources and not the only one if you do not understand markets and withdrawal rates too well.

You can use an SWP in other situations as well. You can specify an amount you want to withdraw or just the profit.

There are funds that allow the trigger facility on the SWP, where you can trigger a redemption that goes to your bank (instead of another scheme as in the STP) according to a formula or market level.

Just because options are there does not mean you need to use them. Sensible mutual fund investing is about narrowing down the huge ocean of options into those that work for you. A simple SWP to fund a defined periodic need is a great option. Watch out for exit loads though. Most equity funds charge you an exit load (explained on page 116 in Chapter 6) to redeem before 365 days; therefore, set up your SWP a year before you need the money so that you are not charged the load.

Forms of holding a mutual fund: demat or non-demat

Have you seen a mutual fund certificate? I am old enough to have held a physical UTI Mastergain 1992 certificate in my hand! In the early years of the mutual fund industry when UTI was the monopoly mutual fund, it used physical certificates, much like the physical share certificates. The problem of matching signatures in sales and the physical problem of certificates getting lost or damaged made the process very clunky, time consuming and expensive. Once the private sector was allowed in, the physical certificates gave way to account statements. This is called holding in physical form but through a statement of account. You buy directly from the fund house or through distributors and banks. You can also buy through a platform now directly from the fund house.

The statement of account is a simple record of your holding and transactions each month. You can also now get a consolidated account statement (CAS) across all your holdings in different mutual funds. Search the internet for ways to access your CAS through your distributor, advisor or directly from CAMS and Kfintech (the registrars and transfer agents).

From 2009, investors got an option to hold mutual fund units in a demat form. You will need a demat account and choose the demat option on the platform as you get to the buying stage. A demat account will cost you an annual fee. You will need to sign up through a depository participant. There will be broker costs to buy and sell mutual fund units—something that you do not pay when you buy directly from the fund house. The setting up of SIPs, STPs and SWPs might be difficult via the demat route. This route is meant for distributors and corporate agents to set up their own platforms that will then offer these services. Each layer that you add between yourself and the mutual fund will eventually end up costing you something, even though it may be free today. The ETF investing requires a demat account and so do some direct bond purchases.

What to use: go for the direct holding with the mutual fund in the form of an account statement. It is lower cost and has all the entry and exit options mentioned in this chapter.

This is the end of a long journey where we looked at entry and exit options. At least initially when getting introduced to mutual funds, it helps to keep it simple and use the basic options rather than go for complicated strategies on trigger- and formula-based investing.

We come to the very important topic of costs and returns in the next chapter. Get a paper and pen if you don't already have one. Treat this not as a lazy Sunday afternoon read, but study material. We are working hard today to make our money work harder in the future.

It is very important to get the choices right before you begin the process of investing in mutual funds. Innovation in the industry has resulted in a large number of options that you need to decide on at the point of scheme purchase.

You are doing okay if you understand that

1. open-ended funds are usually the best option as it prevents a lock-in;
2. the growth option is better than the income-distribution option;
3. a sensible SWP is a better option, under most conditions, to an income-distribution option;
4. the direct option, instead of a regular one, saves you the ongoing trail commission embedded in the expense ratio;
5. an SIP is a great way to match savings and investment rhythm; and
6. an STP is a good way to turn a lump sum into an SIP.

6

COSTS, RETURNS AND BENCHMARKS

Nothing in itself is good or bad. It is all relative. As in life, so also in returns on your investments.

Financial products are invisible and are created in your mind as they are described by the person selling it. It is in the interest of the agent to talk up the good points and omit talking about costs that will impact your real return. You have inflation, taxes and product costs attacking your money from three sides. While the impact of tax is visible, both inflation and product costs are silent killers of return.

We will see the face of the various costs associated with mutual funds now and find out how to carefully choose products that are lower cost. The cheapest product might not be the best because there are other attributes, like risk and return, that we need to look at as well before we finally choose a scheme.

There are various costs related to the entry, maintenance and exit from a mutual fund. Some of these charges are no longer there as they were removed some years back and some of them are new. Indian mutual funds probably have the most transparent cost structure in the world, but this journey has taken the time and effort of a multitude of people associated with this industry—regulators, media and analysts among them. What follows is not just the relevant costs, but also the story of how we got here.

Costs of entry

Mutual funds in India are no-load products. This means that there is no sales charge or commission embedded in the price of the mutual fund unit. When you buy at an NAV of Rs 10, you are not paying a hidden sales commission of Rs 2 that goes to the agent, with only Rs 8 going to work as an investment. But it was not always so. When UTI was a monopoly, the agents would get a sales commission of 5 per cent. Once the industry opened up, the norm became a front sales charge or load of 2.25 per cent, although the SEBI limits earlier allowed a load of 7 per cent across both entry and exit.

What do you pay as an entry load when you invest in a fixed deposit? Nothing. The Rs 5 lakh you invest goes fully to work and your interest is calculated on the entire money. What do you pay as entry cost when you buy a property? The broker's fee, which is usually between 0.5 per cent to

2 per cent of the value of the property. What do you pay as entry cost in an endowment or money-back policy? A huge 35–42 per cent of your premium. That is, of the Rs 5 lakh, up to Rs 2.1 lakh goes straight to the agent who sells you the policy. Mutual funds invest the entire amount without any commission. You do pay a tiny tax each time you invest in the form of a 0.005 per cent stamp duty that was introduced in Budget 2020. Of the Rs 1 lakh you invest, Rs 5 goes to the Union government and Rs 99,995 gets invested.

But before we come to how mutual funds lost the load to benefit the investor, I must tell you the 6 per cent NFO charge story in detail. Till the year 2006, there was another big cost that investors used to pay—the new fund offer (NFO) charge. Mutual funds were allowed to charge investors 6 per cent of the amount they raised during an NFO. A Rs 1,000 crore NFO collection allowed the mutual fund to harvest out Rs 60 crore. This was 'amortized' or spread over five years and charged to the investors. This charge was meant to take care of the costs of bringing the scheme to the market and paying for the initial advertising and distribution costs. During the bull run of 2003–06, mutual funds went on an NFO launch spree and all kinds of funds were brought to market, many times with the intention of harvesting these charges. The distribution community soon joined the game and began to extract a larger and larger share of this 6 per cent. Each time they would sell a new fund to an investor, they would get this extra commission. Add to this the 2.25 per cent load and agents were making over 8 per cent each time they sold a new fund. This resulted in investors being moved in and out of funds just to harvest the commissions. A rising market hid the impact of this cost from investors, but in terms of extra cost, they would have paid a few hundreds of crores over the four-year period ending 2006.

How do I know this? I was working as a consulting editor with *The Indian Express* during this period and had newly passed my CFP certification that armed me with tools to figure out what was going on. The excel sheet proved to be a very powerful tool that prevented lawsuits by angry corporate agents. I remember being yelled at by the CEO of one firm that shall remain unnamed (but I do still remember you!) for the stories we did in *Express*!

Anyhow, the paper ran a series of front-page stories that nailed the 'churning' of investor money that benefited the agents but not the investors. The then SEBI chairman M. Damodaran took note and banned the NFO charges on open-ended funds. I remember a call with him during this time where I said that the industry will switch to close-ended funds. He said, 'They are good boys and will behave.' Turns out I was right, and just before he demitted office in 2008, he banned the charge on close-ended funds as well.

The next charge to come into the regulatory gaze was the front load that had settled at 2.25 per cent of the invested amount. Front loads that are embedded in the price of the financial product encourage agents to sell the higher commission products and then churn the funds to harvest the front load every one or two years. In 2009, the then regulator,

C.B. Bhave, removed these charges and made India the first country to offer all funds with a zero-sales charge embedded in the price of the product. He asked a simple question to see who should compensate the distributor before he took the drastic regulatory step: whose agent is he? If he is the agent of the investor, then the investor must pay. But if he is the agent of the mutual fund, then they need to pay out of their share of the investor's money that they charge as annual costs.

He gave less than half a year for mutual funds to remove this charge. The industry was on fire. Experts predicted the demise of the Indian mutual fund industry. This is a push product, nobody is going to pay separately to invest in a risky product. This is going against the grain of the market. The investors will get no service. On and on the hair pulling and chest beating went. Anyhow, the action was taken and since 2009 to today, the industry has had exponential growth. When things are done in investors' interest, they get to know and begin to trust the product more and more. This is exactly what happened, though it took a long time of investor education and performance for this trust to build.

How do I know this? I was now in the Ministry of Finance on a short stint advising the Swarup Committee that was set up by the government to look into issues of investor protection and financial literacy.[1] It was during the process of this committee that SEBI thought through this issue responding to the questions we raised about commissions and their harmful impact on investors' money and confidence.

Other than a stamp duty tax that costs the investor 0.005 per cent of the investment amount (read Chapter 8 for taxes and their impact), there is no hidden cost during the purchase process of a mutual fund. Distributors can charge Rs 100 or Rs 150 for new investors and this is paid by the mutual fund to the sellers upfront after deducting the investor's account. This charge is not really relevant for most investors.

Banks and platforms can have transaction charges but these are not embedded in the NAV of the fund. You should see them separately as additional charges.

Costs of exit

Exit loads are a cost you pay to the mutual fund at the point of redemption. Not all funds charge this and not all funds charge the same amount. An exit load of 1 per cent will reduce your redemption amount by that much. If you were redeeming Rs 5 lakh, you will get Rs 4.95 lakh in hand. These are imposed to nudge investors to stay invested and discourage churning. Typically, equity funds have a 1 per cent exit load to prevent investors from exiting before a year. This is also a reminder to investors to stay invested for more than a year at least to take advantage of a lower long-term capital gains tax. Read more about this tax in Chapter 8. Some funds will lower the exit load as the holding period rises.

The fund categories of overnight, liquid and ultra-short-term funds have no exit loads, neither typically do banking and PSU and gilt funds. Other debt funds will have a small exit load. You must check for an exit load when you are setting up an STP. And you must check for it when investing in any fund category to not be taken by surprise.

Costs of maintenance: expense ratio

Mutual funds make money even when you don't. You pay an annual management fee to the AMC for managing your money. In Chapter 2, I described the advantages of being able to hire a professional fund manager for a small fee. Had you employed such a team yourself, it might have costed you more than what you are investing. The rules allow for all costs incurred by the AMC and their profits to collect under one head called 'expense ratio'.

An expense ratio is a percentage of your assets under management that is deducted by the fund house towards its costs and profits. An AMC sets up the business, hires offices, hires people for fund management, analysts, admin staff, support staff and needs to pay for all these in-house costs. There are costs of hired services such as fees to registrar and transfer agents, custodians, trustees and lawyers. I won't waste time explaining each of these—they are an internet search away. The purpose is to give you a system to invest and not get caught in minute operational details. The expense ratio also includes the commissions paid to brokers and distributors for selling the funds. With no front loads in the product, the agents selling the funds need to be compensated for the business they bring to the fund house. Their commission is now a part of the expense ratio and is called a trail commission, or commission that trails the product rather than an upfront one. A trail commission works better for all parts of the market as it puts incentives in the right place. This ratio also includes the profits made by the AMC.

SEBI fixes ceilings on this expense ratio—this means that schemes have limits to what they can charge the investors' money. When you look for the expense ratio of a mutual fund, it gives one number, say, 1.5 per cent or 0.45 per cent, but the way the expense ratio is calculated depends on the size of the assets under management of that particular scheme.

The current waterfall of costs can be seen in Table 6.1.

Table 6.1

Expense ratios for open-ended schemes		
AUM (daily net assets)	Cost as a % of daily net assets	
	Equity (%)	Other than equity (%)
First Rs 500 crore	2.25	2.00
Next Rs 250 crore	2.00	1.75
Next Rs 1,250 crore	1.75	1.50
Next Rs 3,000 crore	1.60	1.35
Next Rs 5,000 crore	1.50	1.25
On the next Rs 40,000 crore	TER reduction of 0.05% for every Rs 5,000 crore rise in net assets	
Assets more than Rs 50,000 crore	1.05	0.80

It is a strange-looking table, but we need to understand the numbers and what they mean. Remember that costs are silent killers of returns long term and while this is not the only metric for choosing a scheme, it is an important one. The charging of expense ratios based on AUM level began with the setting up of mutual fund rules in 1996. The expense ratios were higher than the ones you see in this table, with equity cost starting at 2.50 per cent for the first Rs 100 crore, with assets above Rs 700 crore having a ceiling of 1.75 per cent. The logic of a reducing cost as AUM rises is this: unlike a manufacturing firm of real goods and services, the costs of fund management do not increase as the AUM rises. A carmaker will have to spend more on raw material, parts, assembly lines and staff as the production of cars increases. But a rising AUM will have most of the costs as fixed with ever-rising profit margins. The cost of fund management does not rise as AUM rises therefore we see the cost ceilings going down as the assets under management go up for a scheme.

How to read Table 6.1

Think of an equity mutual fund scheme that has Rs 2,000 crore in AUM. The first Rs 500 crore can charge the highest slab expense ratio of 2.25 per cent, the next Rs 250 crore will charge 2 per cent, the next 1,250 crore will charge 1.75 per cent. The expense ratio charged to the scheme therefore is 1.91 per cent.

Another scheme has Rs 60,000 crore in assets under management. This will charge 2.25 per cent for the first Rs 500 crore and so on till it hits the last Rs 10,000 crore that it will charge 1.05 per cent on. The average expense ratio that you will see in your account statement will be 1.29 per cent. Incidentally, that means an annual revenue of Rs 776 crore for the fund house from just this scheme!

Notice that as the fund size has increased, the average expense ratio has dropped. When you see a number against expense ratio in your account statement, you now know how it got there. The smaller the AUM, the larger will be the average expense ratio. Which is why some fund houses try and keep the size of some of their schemes to less than Rs 1,000 crore to harvest the higher costs.

Debt funds have a lower expense ratio as the costs in managing a bond portfolio are assumed to be lower and also, since returns are lower in debt products, the costs have been kept 0.25 percentage points lower. Typically, debt funds (since they are bought more by institutions, corporate treasuries and high net worth individuals—all of whom have bargaining power) fall very quickly down from the regulatory ceilings. The same is not seen in equity, which is a largely retail product.

The costs of the other products were also lowered in the 2019 regulatory action.

Table 6.2

Expense ratio limits	
I. Close-ended and interval funds	Cost as a % of daily net assets
a. Equity	1.25
b. Other than equity	1

Expense ratio limits	
II. Index and ETFs	1%
III. Fund of funds	Cost ceiling includes the cost of the underlying scheme (%)
a. Liquid, index, ETF	1.00
b. Equity	2.25
c. Other than equity	2

While these are the regulatory limits, the actual expense ratio can be much lower. Look out for the size of the scheme that you are buying and if it is larger than Rs 10,000 crore, but expense ratios are still hugging the regulatory limit on expenses, try and get a cheaper fund, with other things like risk and return remaining the same. We will revisit this when we choose schemes in Chapter 10.

Why did SEBI reduce expenses?

You might ask, why did the regulator have to change expense ratios in 2019? SEBI had to intervene because the forces of free markets were not working to the advantage of investors in the mutual fund industry. Both profit margins and distributor commissions were rising at the cost of investors who were not getting a lower price. When the expense ratio limits were fixed in 1996, the size of the mutual fund industry was tiny; by end 1999, the industry AUM was just Rs 97,028 crore. A decade later, in 2009, the AUM was Rs 6.65 trillion. And in 2018 (just before SEBI's reduction of expenses) it was Rs 22.85 trillion. The regulatory and policy thought was that as the industry grew in size, competition would force expense ratios to fall.

But that did not happen and a SEBI public document nails the evidence.[2] One paragraph from that document is worth reproducing here:

> Certain practices followed by some industry participants viz varied practices of charging TER to the scheme; paying commissions from the books of the Asset Management Company (AMC) of the MF and charging the same to the scheme as AMC fees resulting in defraying the cost on direct investors; subverting the spirit of regulations by launching an increasing number of close ended schemes, apart from impacting the overall TER, have resulted in unhealthy environment for the mutual fund industry. Such practices have also resulted in mis-selling and unnecessary churn in the investors' portfolio.

I often hear the argument that India has regulatory overreach and SEBI gets into micro-managing the industry. What you, as an investor with no lobby working for you, need to know is that the job of a good regulator is to look after your interest since market forces, especially in finance, do not. The expense ratio story is a great example of this.

What happened is this: as the AUM rose over the decades, the margins increased for the mutual fund industry since cost does not rise pro rata in the financial sector. The profit margins rose from almost 19 per cent in 2010–11 to just over 35 per cent by 2017–18. The SEBI documents that in retail-heavy categories like equity funds, expense ratios remained near the regulatory ceiling, but in institutional and corporate heavy categories like debt funds, the expense ratios dropped sharply. Where was the money that should have been shared with the investor going? Into higher and higher distributor commissions. The commission paid from AMC profits rose from 11 per cent over 2009–10 to a huge 22 per cent in 2017–18.

Therefore the 2019 regulation to reduce expense ratios. Why is there that strange-looking 1.05 per cent—why not round it off to a 1 per cent? The reduction of expense ratios was a protracted negotiation between SEBI and the industry. How do I know? I was part of the subcommittee that worked on reducing the expense ratios. All I can document here is that each five basis points of lower expense ratio was hotly debated. The last 0.05 per cent became a tipping point that would have derailed the months and months of work that had already gone into the process. So, we went with the 1.05 per cent and not 1 per cent! By the way, that 0.05 per cent will mean crores of revenue for the AMCs who reach a certain size. Why do you need to know this? When regulations come out suddenly, the process is not so well understood. It is not that SEBI woke up one morning and changed the ratios in a totally arbitrary manner. No, this took months of consultation, negotiation, arguments with the industry and then finally a consensus.

What you need to remember is this: expenses matter to us as investors and having understood how much meat there is on the bone for the fund houses, we as investors must make them earn the higher charges for active funds. Passive funds have lower limits and expense ratios. Index funds and ETFs can charge a maximum of 1 per cent expense, but this part of the market has seen costs fall sharply. The cheapest index fund (not ETF, those are cheaper but you will need to pay brokerage and other costs) costs you just 0.06 per cent. The names of the cheapest index funds will keep changing as the industry gets more competitive, but the message to you is very clear: if you are in an active fund, ensure that the fund manager is earning the extra cost you will pay by giving you a return that is at least 4 per cent to 5 per cent higher than the benchmark return, else stay with a very cheap index fund.

As the mutual fund industry grows in the next decade, look out for more regulatory action in reducing both the expense ratios and possibly the trail commissions that are sitting at a fat 1 per cent of your assets under management.

NAV

Net asset value or NAV is the price per unit of a mutual fund scheme. It is the price at which you enter and exit a scheme. It measures the value of the portfolio minus the costs. A new fund offers units at Rs 10 per unit. Suppose it collects Rs 1,000 crore by selling 100 crore units. Ignoring all costs at this point, the mutual fund buys stocks and bonds from this money and after a month, the assets grow to Rs 1,050 crore. The stocks and bonds it bought grew by Rs 50 crore. How will this reflect in your holding? The Rs 1,050 crore amount will get divided by the number of units outstanding (ignoring any fresh purchase or sale of units) and the new price of a unit is Rs 10.50. After a year, if the AUM is Rs 2,000 crore due to the rise in the value of the stocks and bonds, it will take the price of a unit to Rs 20.

How does the portfolio grow? Because the value of the stocks and bonds has increased, and this is called the undistributed profit. Undistributed because the fund has not released this money to the investor in the growth plan, though it might do so in the IDCW plan. The other ways the mutual fund earns is through interest on the bonds it holds, through dividend it receives on shares. When the companies issue rights and bonus shares, those get added to the portfolio as well. So, the value of your money in the fund grows as it receives dividend, interest and makes profits. But all of that money does not belong to you—you need to pay for the costs of the mutual fund, that all sit beneath the expense ratio. These costs are deducted every day so that you can see the value of your money, net of costs, every day.

Hence, *net* asset value.

If the expense ratio is 2 per cent, then on a daily basis, 2 per cent divided by 365 is charged to the fund and your asset value adjusts for this. Mutual funds are 'marked to market' every day, which means the value of the portfolio is disclosed every day to show the gains and the losses. Of course, long-term equity investors need not track the NAV every day but once in six months to check on how your investments are doing. The NAV is disclosed every day for another reason—investors can sell their holdings and new investors can come in to buy every day that the market is open. Both need a price that reflects the value of the portfolio on that day. Hence the daily NAV.

The declaration of a daily NAV prevents hiding the lack of performance of a scheme from investors and continues to give a true picture of the value of investor money. Dark pools of money that are not marked to market can give rise to poor or conflicted investment decisions.

You must note two things about the NAV. One, when we calculate returns later on in this chapter, what we will get is net returns since the costs of fund management have already been accounted for in the NAV. So, when you compare NAV across time for the same scheme, it is possible to get a handle on the post-cost growth of your money. The same cannot be said of a product like the unit linked insurance plan (ULIP) that has costs such as the mortality cost (what the pure life insurance part costs) outside of the NAV.

Two, a Rs 10 NAV is in no way better or cheaper than a Rs 450 NAV. There was a time in the history of mutual funds that distributors, especially during the churning scam period 2003 to 2008, were using the Rs 10 NAV of a new fund to make investors switch from their older schemes that might have had a higher NAV. Their argument was that, look, Rs 10 is cheaper isn't it? And the potential for appreciation will be higher when the NAV is lower. If you have understood the product by now, you would know why this logic is so badly flawed. Not understood? Okay, let me explain: both the Rs 10 NAV new fund and the older Rs 450 NAV fund (if their portfolios are exactly the same) will be impacted in exactly the same way by a market rise or fall. Remove the noise of costs and taxes for a minute and look at a 10 per cent rise in the underlying shares that both hold in exactly the same proportion. A 10 per cent gain will move the NAV from Rs 10 to Rs 11, and from Rs 450 to Rs 495—both will gain 10 per cent.

The mutual fund's value is due to the shares, bonds, gold and their combinations that they hold. It is a pass-through that simply uses your money to buy these assets. A share gathers premium over its lifetime, a mutual fund does not—its NAV simply reports the value of the portfolio today divided by the number of units outstanding.

The SEBI rules make it mandatory for every scheme to declare its NAV by 11 p.m. every day. For fund of funds, the deadline is 10 a.m. the following morning. The NAVs are usually updated by 10 p.m. on the AMFI site.[3]

What NAV you get when you invest or redeem depends on the time of your order and the money reaching the fund house. Called cut-off time, this deadline determines which day's NAV you will get when you buy or sell.

Other than overnight and liquid funds, if you place the buy order and get the money to the fund house before 3 p.m.

you get that day's NAV. If your order or money reaches the fund house post this cut off time, you will get the NAV of the next working day. For a sale order placed before 3 p.m., you get the same day's NAV; after 3 p.m., you get the next day's NAV.

For overnight and liquid funds, the cut-off times are different. If the order and funds are available in a buy order before 1.30 p.m., you get the previous day's NAV. If the funds are available after 1.30 p.m., you get the same day's NAV. For a sale order placed before 3 p.m., same day's NAV and after 3 p.m., next day's NAV.

You need to know the rules, but one day here or there in NAV will make little difference to a long-term equity investor. The NAV values matter a lot to entities like corporate treasuries, institutions and very high net worth investors where even a few basis points of variance in the NAV will result in crores of rupees of difference. My suggestion is to not stress too much on timing the NAV exactly, and the SIP regime releases you from the pressure of getting the best NAV. There is never a best. Markets keep moving up and down, and over a long enough holding period these differences get ironed out.

The NAV at which you buy and sell will be different to the extent of the exit load in the product. An exit load of 1 per cent will make the NAV that much lower when you sell. If the NAV is Rs 300 and there is a 1 per cent exit load, your applicable NAV will be Rs 297.

The last thing to note is this: the NAV by itself gives you no information, but it is the comparison of the NAV over time that gives you a handle of return. Which is what we will do next.

Return

A mutual fund is a pass-through entity. All the funds belong to the investors and other than the expense ratio, a mutual fund is not allowed to dip into investor money at all. Therefore, the entire return belongs to the investor and is reflected in the changing NAV over time. If the NAV moves from Rs 10 to Rs 50 over a period of three years, then the return has been 400 per cent over the period. On an annual basis it has been 71 per cent return.

But where does the return come from? It comes from the underlying portfolio of stocks, bonds, gold and combinations of these that the mutual fund holds. A return is earned in three ways—interest, dividend and profit. Interest on the bonds the portfolio holds. Dividend on the stocks it holds. Profit will come from the gains on prices on stocks, bonds and gold held in the portfolio.

How we count return and then what metrics we use become important as we get ready to start choosing mutual fund schemes. We will see in Chapter 12 why the scheme that gave the highest return last year may not be the best for you. But first we need to understand the various measures of return. In the example above, the 400 per cent return certainly looks better than the 71 per cent return, but both are giving you the same return, except in the first case you took a point-to-point return and disregarded the number of years in the middle. This is usually how endowment plans are sold—your Rs 1 lakh becomes Rs 5 lakh. They omit to tell you that this conversion happens over a twenty-year period if you stay in the product. The second measure, also called a compounded annual growth rate or CAGR, is a much better measure for it considers the number of years it took your Rs 10 to turn to Rs 50. The CAGR for the endowment plan is just 8.4 per cent.

Using point-to-point returns is also how we evaluate our real estate investments. I've heard this said so often: 'My Rs 30 lakh property became worth Rs 2 crore—such a great return!'

What they do not say is that this journey happened over a thirty-year period, giving a CAGR of 6.5 per cent. Did you know that the CAGR on the Sensex over thirty years has been 14.5 per cent?

The way that mutual fund returns are most often shown is through trailing returns. It gives the past CAGR return history over a time period you can define. Most often we see trailing returns over the past one, three, five, seven, ten, fifteen and twenty years. Each day that you look at the trailing returns, they can look different since they are being calculated with the latest NAV over the past period we select. Trailing returns give a good handle on consistency of performance and we will learn how to use these trailing returns to choose schemes in Chapter 10. But trailing returns have a flaw—they hide the true performance of a scheme over various time periods within a year itself. It will hide the volatility, or the sharp up and down movements of the NAV during the year.

Another way to look at returns over a long period of time is to use rolling returns. This method shows the investor experience over the entire period chosen. It is a difficult concept that I have explained in *Let's Talk Money* in Chapter 8—do refresh from there.

Essentially, rolling returns tell us the worst and the best performance history of a scheme. It maps the return history as if the investment happened every day of the year (to take away the timing bias) and then held for a one, two, three or longer period of time. Rolling return helps to identify the return consistency of a fund.

We will use a combination of trailing returns, with some risk metrics and expense ratios to finally select funds in Chapter 10. An additional check can be done using a rolling return calculator (an internet search is your friend for this!) for those who want to be extra sure and want to do some more work.

Benchmark

'That person is very tall.' If you heard this statement in India, you would imagine a man who is over five feet six inches tall. If you heard this in the Netherlands, you would imagine a man who is over six feet tall. In Guatemala, a woman would need to be over four feet eleven inches in height to be considered tall. A tall Guatemalan woman would be considered below average height in the Netherlands where the average is five feet seven inches.

Height, by itself, tells us nothing about the tallness of a person. It depends on where they are and what the average height in that place is. Returns also need a context, an average, a benchmark to be useful to us as a metric for choosing a fund.

For example, Taurus Largecap Fund Direct (data on 6 April 2023) showed a three-year return of 18.97 per cent CAGR. Looks great, you think. But look at the benchmark for the fund, the S&P BSE 100 total return index (TRI) that saw a return of 25.96 per cent and the large-cap category average which was 22.26 per cent. An actively managed fund that charges 2.49 per cent a year in expense ratio needs to beat the benchmark to justify the higher risk active funds take over passive funds. You would have been better off in an index fund on the same index with a fraction of the cost.

We use benchmarks in mutual funds to tell us the extent to which the scheme is outperforming or underperforming. We use them as a standard against which to measure performance.

Till 2018, most funds would use an easier benchmark to show a higher outperformance of their funds. But from 1 February 2018, SEBI mandated that the benchmarks are a total return index rather than a price return index (PRI). A PRI only captures the capital gains (profits) of the securities (stocks and bonds) that it tracks. The total return index also counts interest, dividends along with the capital gains. You would have understood that a total return index will be higher than a PRI because it now includes more items of return. Fund houses would use the PRI to make their schemes look better than they actually were. The TRI would typically show returns that were about 1.5 percentage points higher than the PRI. So, a fund giving a three-year return of 11 per cent would outperform a PRI that showed a three-year return at 10 per cent, but not when compared to the TRI that mapped a 11.5 per cent return. Some fund houses were using the TRI even before the SEBI rule, but it needed regulatory action to bring uniformity in the market.

The choice of benchmarks was left to the fund houses. But from 1 January 2022, SEBI has specified the benchmarks that each of the thirty-seven categories of funds must use. The regulator again wanted to bring uniformity in the industry so that an investor can choose a fund without worrying about what benchmark the fund might be using. SEBI allowed for two benchmarks for some categories because the fund managers wanted to benchmark returns according to their investment style.

The first benchmark in all categories is specified by SEBI and funds can choose one index provider out of the current four that are in the market. For example, the large-cap category can choose either the Nifty 100 or the S&P BSE 100 TRI as a benchmark. A conservative hybrid fund can choose either the Nifty 50 Hybrid Composite Debt 15:85 index or the CRISIL Hybrid 85+15 conservative index.[4]

Do not worry too much about the benchmark since SEBI has put the rules under the bonnet and you can just look at the benchmark displayed by the scheme without fear of being manipulated.

Why a second-tier benchmark? A second-tier benchmark reflects the investment style of the fund manager within the category. Again, when the benchmark discussion was happening between the regulator and the industry, the fund managers did not want SEBI to specify a benchmark saying that it cramped their style and was not reflective of the investment philosophy of a particular fund. The purpose of the second index is to allow the fund manager to showcase the ability to beat a subcategory of the benchmark—for example, a portfolio that only has triple A rated bonds over a more mixed portfolio. A more mixed portfolio might have higher return, but will also carry higher risk. Another fund manager might want to run a large-cap fund with a focus on the top fifty stocks out of 100 (remember that the first 100 stocks makes the large-cap category—go to page 49 in Chapter 4 to see the market cap limits again) and another one might want a focus on the last fifty—both will be able to choose second-tier benchmarks that reflect their own subcategory of a larger category they have fixed or some other investment style that they choose. SEBI does not specify the second-tier benchmark but lets the funds choose their own.

Who makes the benchmarks? There are now firms such as NSE Indices (owned by the National Stock Exchange) and Asia Index Pvt. Ltd (joint venture of BSE and S&P Dow Jones index) that specialize in constructing, maintaining and selling the use of these indices. Mutual funds need to buy the license to use the index they want to use. A part of the expense ratio of index funds and ETFs goes to pay these licensing fees. There are four index providers that funds can use. The regulator is now at the brink of regulating the index providers because they can get up to some sharp tricks as well. An update to this book will map those regulations in the future. I think I will need to do new editions regularly given the pace of the innovations in the industry and the regulations by SEBI, so watch out for updated editions along the way.

Remember that each extra benchmark the fund house is using, it is adding to the expense ratio in the license fee it pays to the index providers. I like to keep it simple. I look at the Sensex and Nifty 50 return, then the category benchmark return, and then the average category return to evaluate the performance of the scheme.[5]

While newbie investors just look at return when they invest, and go wrong most of the times, the smarter investors look at many other attributes of a scheme. The most important part that you must never let go out of sight is risk. And that's where we head to overleaf. Tank up for another intense bout.

Costs are important in a financial product because it is invisible. It is possible to hide costs using jargon. Mutual fund returns will be lower in higher cost products; therefore, it is important to know what these are and where to find them.

You are doing okay if you understand that

1. other than a .005 per cent stamp duty, there is no cost of entry into a mutual fund;
2. annual expense ratios are limited and most funds will charge below that;
3. equity has higher expense ratios than debt;
4. index funds have very low expense ratios;
5. an NAV of 10 is not cheaper than an NAV of 250; and
6. benchmarks are very important to judge returns.

7

RISK

If an investment looks too good to be true, it is too good to be true.

'I want high return and no risk' is a utopian-investor ask. We need to understand two key things about risk. One, there is never going to be high return without higher risk. Those who promise risk-free high returns are lying. There is no kinder way to put it. The crypto 'currency' stories that promised untold wealth did not talk about the risk of your money evaporating in a fraud-driven non-regulated industry that rose up from dust and is sinking back into it. Two, there are many kinds of risk—and not just the risk of volatility or the sharp up and down movement of price in a short period of time—that we need to consider while making an investment.

Is there a chance that the airplane you are in will crash? Yes, there is. Do you take flights? Yes, you do. You tell yourself that the probability of an air crash is lower than that of a road accident. One MIT professor actually wrote a paper on this.[1] He wrote: 'The risk is so low that being afraid to fly is a little like being afraid to go into the supermarket because the ceiling might collapse.' And flying commercial is still safer than chartered and own aircraft. There are lessons here for us investors, but let's come to that a bit later.

Is there a chance that you might get food poisoning when you eat that plate of aloo tikki off the road? Yes, there is. Do you eat it? Of course! But you go the usual place where you have been eating for years without an incident. In a new place, you do look at the outlet and see if the guy serving has dirty hands or that the cloth he uses to wipe the plate was just now being used to wipe the counter. So, you do some basic checks, but don't put your life on hold because of a possible risk of ill health.

Was there a risk of getting COVID-19 when the pandemic was at its furious worst in April and May 2021 in India? Yes, there was a big risk, but you stayed home, wore masks for any mandatory public visit like to the store, disinfected delivered stuff and took the vaccine. You did what you could to mitigate the risk and yet some of us caught that mean Delta bug.

Risk in investing needs to be unpacked much more than what we think it is. Off the cuff, most people say 'I want no risk to my money. I like fully guaranteed returns.' So do I, but there is a cost of a guarantee that we forget we pay. That cost is a return so low that your money does not stay ahead of inflation and taxes.

I want you to see the various faces of risk and see how to deal with them over your investment journey. There is never a perfect product that will keep you safe from all the risks, but some options do better than others in dealing with most of the risks I cover here.

Inflation

Inflation is called a silent killer of purchasing power, or what your money can buy. A 5 per cent inflation rate over ten years will make prices go up in a compounded manner. What happens to your returns also happens to prices—the price rise each year sits on top of the price rise in the previous year and on and on. The FD rate is usually just below or just above the inflation rate. The rate of return after adjusting for the impact of inflation is called the *real rate* of return.

Nominal return is what you get in rupees in your hand. Real return is what that money can actually buy after you take into account the price rise over the holding period. If the return is 5 per cent and inflation is at 6 per cent, you have lost around a percentage point of purchasing power. Add the tax on interest that you pay on slab level (more on this in Chapter 8) and you have a lower return number.

A good investment is one that keeps the purchasing power of your money, post tax, ahead of inflation. Most fixed-income products like FDs do very well on safety, but do not keep your money ahead of inflation. In India the provident fund and public provident fund are outliers in this since their annual returns have kept ahead of inflation. And since they are tax free, they make for a good core for the debt part of your portfolio. More on this in Chapter 12 where we use these products to make model portfolios.

Other than these two products, it is not a good idea to keep your long-term money in debt instruments that do worse than inflation.

Market risk

You would have heard the hurried disclaimer: 'mutualfundsaresubjecttomarketrisk….' Market risk is also called *systemic risk*, or the risk that cannot be reduced by diversification. All others kinds of risk that we are discussing in this chapter come under the umbrella of *unsystematic risk*, or specific risks that can be reduced through diversification. How does systemic risk impact you? Remember when, in March of 2020, the COVID-19–related panic caused a large crash in the stock market and even the bond markets were near freezing? The only asset that grew in price was gold—seen as the last resort to an end-of-the-world scenario. For such a total catastrophic event, you need to have a stash of emergency funds that is very liquid. But don't overthink this and rush to hoarding cash or gold. If the world ends, then no amount of gold is of use to you or your family. But if you survive and so does most of humanity, then we will quickly get back to consuming and producing stuff. Markets will get back on track after a period of instability and panic. For that interim period of distress, you need cash or near cash assets like gold.

When the Sensex crashed down to 29,000 in March 2020, many investors lost their nerve and sold off their entire equity portfolios not knowing how much worse this could get. My view was this: we will not go back to caves and wheelbarrows, this crisis will eventually end, and if your basic asset allocation was sensible, this is absolutely not the time to sell equity.

Face the fact that, just as in life, major and minor crises will appear suddenly but they do tend to go away after a bit. So also with markets—they get back on track once a crisis blows over. For the last two decades there has been a new crisis each year, starting from Y2K, to the North Atlantic Financial crisis, then the European crisis, COVID-19 and then the Russia–Ukraine war. We need to take them in our stride and not allow them to freeze our investments with a rush to safety. I know people who did that in April 2020, and three years later are still waiting for a break in the markets to reenter. You deal with market risk by having a well-diversified portfolio—across stocks and bonds—that matches your age, stage, distance of goals from today and risk capacity. These are just words that mean nothing till we put them to use, which we will in Chapter 12.

Interest rate risk

This is the risk of a change in interest rate affecting bond prices. Bond prices move up when interest rates move down and they move down when interest rates go up. Your FD is not a marketable security, which means you cannot trade your FD on a stock market. But bonds are now mostly listed on a stock exchange and are tradeable. A change in interest rates causes a change in bond prices in the secondary market where bond trading takes place. If the central bank raises rates, then bond prices will fall as investors rush to buy the new bonds that offer a higher interest. If the central bank reduces rates, then buyers rush to buy the older bonds that have a now-higher interest than the new bonds.

This relationship between interest rates and bond prices is measured by a concept called duration. Very simply, duration measures by how much will bond prices change (rise or fall) for a 1 percentage point change (fall or rise) in interest rates. A duration of three years, for example, means that a 1 per cent fall in interest rates will cause a 3 per cent rise in bond prices. What you need to know is that the longer the holding period of the bond or bond portfolio, the greater is the duration and hence the greater is the risk of changes in interest rates, and therefore changes in bond prices.

Your risk is of holding a portfolio of bonds that have an average maturity that is different from your holding period. Average maturity is the average number of days, weeks, months or years that all the bonds in the portfolio will take to mature or pay back the principal. Suppose there are ten bonds in the portfolio and some are maturing in two months and some in three months and some in four months, then the average maturity period will be worked out to give an average number. Remember that the risk to your principal and interest becomes smaller and smaller as the bond comes close to maturity. Therefore, the overnight and liquid funds are considered the safest. But to prevent mutual funds from stuffing different maturity bonds in their portfolio, thereby increasing the interest rate risk, SEBI has put in place rules that match your holding period to the residual average maturity (a two-year bond might have only two months of life left, so the maturity of this bond will be in two months and not in two years—hence *residual* average maturity) of the bond portfolio. Go back to Chapter 4 to see the debt fund categories one more time to understand this better.

Again, SEBI has done a deep clean of the debt part of the market in the late 2010s and early 2020s, so that if you match your holding period to the correct category, your interest rate risk is well managed. Do not buy a long-term bond if you need the money short term, and the reverse is also true.

Credit risk

This is the risk of the borrower not paying interest and principal either on time, or at all. Interest is the price that the borrower of money (through issuing a bond) pays to the lender. The lender needs to be compensated for three things: the risk that the borrower will not return the money, for deferring consumption and the risk of inflation denting purchasing power. The biggest risk for a lender is the possibility that the borrower vanishes with the money.

How do you evaluate this risk? Remember that a bond is a promise by the borrower to the lender to pay a certain rate of interest, at a certain periodicity and the return of principal in exchange for a loan. To create a market where there are unknown lenders and borrowers, the evaluation of the risk of default of both interest and principal, becomes important. How will buyers of bonds understand the risk of thousands of businesses who are borrowing by issuing bonds? This problem was solved by creating credit rating agencies whose job it is to evaluate the business, the risk and then give its 'opinion' on the quality of the paper. This risk is denoted by a series of letters—for example, a triple A rating denotes very low risk to the lender and a D minus rating points to a junk bond.

Government bonds have no credit risk since the government will pay its debts in a solvent state. But corporate bonds can have this risk that can vary from very good quality to very poor. The low-rated corporate bonds will usually offer a much higher rate of interest to compensate the lender for the much higher risk taken. Notice that the category called credit-risk funds can in some years give very high returns. But there are years in which they do really badly.

An average investor who is looking at debt funds for short-term liquidity purposes must not take credit risk in her portfolio. The risk of not having the money when you need it is not worth the return.

Liquidity risk

How easy is it for you to sell your two BHK in a tight time frame in a market where there are few buyers due to an economic slowdown? Distress sales in real estate usually end up with the seller having to take a cut in the price he gets. We can see this as a liquidity risk.

Liquidity is defined as the ease (of time and money) with which an asset can be converted into cash, without affecting its market price. The risk arises when this takes too much time and costs the seller a lot.

Mutual funds do not have this risk because the fund house is obligated to repurchase at NAV. In normal market situations you get the redemption money within one-to-four working days. The ETFs, however, do have this risk present since there needs to be a counterparty buying when you are selling. The lack of a buyer will cause the price to drop and large transactions might be difficult in a thin-demand market. In most situations, this is not a risk you worry about in a mutual fund. An extreme situation such as a global crisis might see small periods of illiquidity, but if you have the ability to just hold on, they pass.

Reinvestment risk

I get this question all the time: should I sell my equity funds; the markets are very high? Apart from being flummoxed at the same question by the same people over the years, I don't get why they don't understand this counter question: what will you do with the money if you sell? Where will you reinvest?

Traditionally, reinvestment risk is seen as the fall in interest rates when your bonds mature and you need to move to a lower return bond than today. But I can extend this to look at all the asset classes to say this: unless there is a need of money or you need to rebalance your portfolio, there is no need to sell a winning asset class just because you have made a profit today. Let's revisit this in Chapter 12 when we create portfolios and understand asset allocation better.

Volatility risk

This is a risk we all understand very well—the risk of prices moving up and down specially over a short period of time. The FDs have no volatility since they do not trade on the secondary market. Typically, a very short-term bond will have much lower volatility than a longer term bond.

Real estate is not volatile, though the listed stocks of real estate companies are. Equity is very sensitive to national, international and company-specific events and can be very volatile. Our efforts in reducing this risk will be focused on how to measure it and how to find metrics that map the upside and downside risk of the portfolios that mutual funds create.

Risk of fraud

This is the risk of somebody running away with your money. Of floating a fraudulent scheme, collecting investor money and then vanishing. India has experienced such events periodically. In the stock market in the 1990s, there was a period of vanishing companies. These would come to the

IPO market, collect hundreds of crores and then simply disappear. Mutual fund rules were made in the aftermath of the stock market scam of 1992 and therefore, it has a water-tight structure where the money is held by a trust in the name of the investor. No sponsor or AMC has run away with investor money. You face market risk, the risk of volatility and all other risks that can be managed, but not the risk of losing your entire invested amount. This is a big safety belt and must not be discounted.

Measuring risk

An investor's dream is very high return with no risk. But we know that utopia exists only in the stories scamsters tell and in the traps they weave for gullible investors. There is nothing in life that is risk free. A person can die from a peanut going down the wrong pipe and there are stories of survivors who wash up after spending days in shark-infested waters in the sea. The no-risk approach is not human—we take controlled risks for everything we do. Even marriage is a huge risk, isn't it? Who knows what the partner turns out to be, but it is not as if that risk is preventing marriages in India.

Let us modify the aforementioned statement of risk-free high return into something achievable. We want to reduce the risk per unit of return we earn. Finance uses the concept of risk-adjusted return to measure this. If two funds give the same return, we want to see which fund took lesser risk to achieve it. You have two options of getting from Delhi to Chandigarh, both take five hours. One is a straight train journey that stops at every station, is slow for a train but gets you there. The other is the road that has many sections that are broken, the truck drivers seem to be on some substance that makes them reckless and the cattle have a habit of suddenly darting across the road making the risk multiply. Both get you there in the same time, but the train journey is far less risky.

Mutual funds are similar. Two funds can show the same five-year CAGR, but how they got there might be very different. We need some way to identify the risk in a portfolio and also find a way to capture the outperformance of the fund manager over just index returns. I will give you some basic metrics of measurement of risk and risk adjusted return without going into the formulas or calculations. These are calculated and given by the fund houses themselves and by analysts that are available online. We need to understand the concept and then see how to use it to evaluate the schemes from which we will choose the one.

Standard deviation

First, we need to measure risk. This is done by a metric called standard deviation. We know the concept of the average, or the standard value. The average height of Indian men is five feet six inches. Standard deviation measures how dispersed, or far away on both sides, the male population of India is. A standard deviation of 1 would mean that 68 per cent of the population will fall between five feet five inches and five feet seven inches. A standard deviation of 2 would mean that 95 per cent of the male population would fall between five feet four inches and five feet eight inches. The six-footer friend of yours is an outlier, beyond even 3 standard deviations that maps 99.7 per cent of the data.

When we measure returns, the standard deviation tells us how far away from the average return our return expectation should be. For example, if a fund's average return is 10 per cent with a standard deviation of 2, then 68 per cent of the times (called 1 standard deviation), the fund's returns will lie in the range of 8 per cent and 12 per cent. And 95 per cent of the times (called 2 standard deviations), the returns will lie between 6 per cent and 14 per cent.

If the standard deviation is 3, the range of returns you can expect goes up. A 1 standard deviation will point to a return range of between 7 per cent and 13 per cent. A 2 standard deviation will point to a return range of 4 per cent and 16 per cent. Do you see how the downside risk is going up as the standard deviation is rising? We don't mind the upside return when standard deviation is high, but we don't like the downside risk.

Another way to understand this is to see that the standard deviation of a liquid fund will be much lower than a credit risk fund. And that of a large-cap fund will be much lower than a small-cap fund.

Too tough? Okay, just remember that a lower standard deviation is less risky than a higher standard deviation. When you compare a set of schemes, with other attributes like return, cost and consistency the same, a lower standard deviation will point to a less risky way to get that return.

Beta

Next, we want to see whether the scheme is giving passive fund returns or if there is outperformance. We want to invest in active funds only if they outperform the benchmark, right? If you don't know why, go back to the costs part and understand this again. The average return we know is measured by the relevant benchmark. Now we want to measure how far from the benchmark are the returns of the scheme. We use beta as a metric to measure this. Not beta as in son, but pronounced 'beeta'. Once somebody on Twitter got very upset with me because I wrote something about beta and they said that I was gender insensitive, what about the girls, he asked? Guy was serious about his rant. We seriously need basic finance for all in schools!

Beta measures how far away from the benchmark is the fund return. It measures the volatility—the risk we all worry about so much. Now we have a way to hold this, to measure this fear in our hearts of returns going up and down. Beta to the rescue. No beti yet in finance. Maybe we rewrite Finance 101? Sorry, bad joke, back to risk!

A beta of 1 means that the fund is giving benchmark returns. A beta less than 1 means the fund is less volatile than the benchmark and a beta greater than 1 means more volatile than the benchmark. A beta of 0.65 means that for a 1 percentage point change in the benchmark, the fund will change by 0.65 per cent. If the benchmark moved up 1 per cent, then the fund will rise by 0.65 per cent. But if the index fell by 1 per cent, the fund will fall by only 0.65 per cent.

A beta of 1.5 would mean that when the index moves up by 1 per cent, the fund will move up by 1.5 per cent, but when the index falls by 1 per cent, our fund would fall by 1.5 per cent. So, a lower beta is less risky than a higher beta. But we also don't want a beta of 1 for our active funds—that means there is no fund manager performance, we are just getting index return—better to be in a low-cost passive fund.

Sharpe ratio

Ideally, we want our scheme to outperform the index or benchmark, but we also want to measure the risk-adjusted return—or to find out if the return came at the cost of too much risk. One measure for this is Sharpe ratio. It considers the risk-free return (for example, your bank FD rate or a government bond price) and calculates the excess return given by the scheme, and then uses standard deviation to divide this to give us a number.

The Sharpe ratio tells us if returns are due to excessive risk or smart fund management.

What you need to know is that a low Sharpe ratio means lower risk-adjusted return and a higher ratio means more returns per unit of risk taken. Higher the risk-adjusted return, higher this ratio. Remember that we are not going to use these ratios in isolation because each of them has limitations.

Sortino ratio

The Sharpe ratio measures both the up and the down volatility. What we want is a measure that gives us the upside without the downside dragging us low too badly. We use the Sortino ratio to measure downside volatility only. A high Sortino ratio tells us that the fund is safer as there is a lower chance of negative volatility. We are getting the excess return for a lower downside risk when markets go down.

What we want is a measure that tells us how the fund performs in up-markets and down-markets, and choose the one that does well when markets go up but does not do so badly when markets go down. See how we are nearing our heart's desire of high return with less risk. You just need to remember that a higher Sortino ratio is good when you compare funds across the same category. Do not make the error of using these ratios to compare across asset classes or even between categories. A small-cap fund will have a much lower Sortino ratio than a large-cap fund. But we need both in our portfolio. Within the small-cap funds shortlisted, we look at Sortino ratio to pick out the fund we finally might select.

Alpha

But we still have not removed the excess risk over the general risk in the market. A measure called alpha comes to the rescue. This measures the extra return of the scheme when compared to the relevant benchmark, for a given amount of risk that the scheme takes.

More simply, it is a measure of the outperformance of the fund manager over the benchmark return. Alpha tells you whether the outperformance of the scheme was due to the fund manager's skill of giving higher risk-adjusted return or due to higher risk. A high alpha tells us that the fund manager is good at her job—both in up-markets and down-markets.

Using the ratios

Again, this is a very bare bones explanation of these metrics, nobody expects you to calculate the ratios and remember the formula for each of them. In the chapter on fund selection, we will understand how to use lists of funds that are already ranked on risk-adjusted returns. We still need to be able to look at the different risk metrics in these shortlisted schemes to further select those with higher risk-adjusted return metrics.

You can use some short-cuts to use these ratios, but remember that in itself, the ratio means nothing. It is in its application that it becomes useful. In the shortlist of funds in the category you have, look out for schemes that have the following attributes *compared* to others:

Standard Deviation—low
Alpha—high
Beta—low
Sharpe ratio—high
Sortino ratio—high

There is another way to mark the risk in a mutual fund scheme. SEBI mandates attaching a Risk-o-Meter to every scheme so that investors better understand the risk of what they are buying. The process began in 2013, when three colours were used to indicate risk. Blue meant that the principal was at low risk (typically debt funds), yellow meant that the principal was at medium risk (typically hybrid funds) and brown meant that the principal was at high risk (all equity funds). This version of the Risk-o-Meter had many flaws. It did not consider the different risk attributes within an asset class. The three levels of risk were not descriptive enough of all the combinations of assets classes and within an asset class that were available.

The year 2015 saw another version of the Risk-o-Meter that had five levels of risk. According to the category that a mutual fund belonged to, the risk attribute was assigned at the time of the NFO. The risk categories were low, moderately low, medium, moderately high and high.

While an improvement over the previous version, this Risk-o-Meter had two existential flaws—it did not map the risk within an asset class and was static to the risk attribute chosen at the time of the NFO.

Debt funds in India went through a crisis period that started around 2015. The first shock to debt fund investors came when in August 2015, JP Morgan Mutual Fund was hit hard by the credit rating downgrade of Amtek Auto. The NAVs of its short-term and ultra-short-term debt fund dropped sharply in a day. The reason was the steep credit rating downgrade of the bonds of Amtek Auto from AA minus to C causing bond prices to fall sharply. Investors use short-term debt funds with the idea that the principal is largely safe and the funds have low credit risk. Retail investors were sold these funds with the verbal assurance of safety with higher returns, but were not told about the risk of lower rated bond papers in the portfolio. The Risk-o-Meter did not capture it.

The JP Morgan Amtek auto story was not an isolated case. Soon the schemes of other mutual funds began to show stress as well. The industry tried to side pocket the contaminated paper as a way to stop the contagion from spreading to the rest of the portfolio, but at best this was a half step. The problem was in the DNA of debt funds not marking all the risks properly in the then current version of the Risk-o-Meter. Another issue with static rating is that the quality of the securities held can change over time even within the category, especially in debt funds. Equity is marked high risk in any case; the problem happens in the risk profiling of debt funds.

There was a related problem with this story—credit rating agencies doing a shoddy job. Amtek Auto's troubles had been in the news for months before the rating agencies at one shot downgraded the paper by several notches. When hauled up by the regulator, the rating agencies took refuge under the fig leaf of ratings being mere opinions and that they cannot be held to account for the trueness of the ratings. The US-based credit rating agencies who had marked junk bonds as triple

A in the years leading up to the North Atlantic Financial Crisis (it is important to not call it the 'global' financial crisis—India and China were not a part of the excesses of Wall Street!) also escaped regulatory and legal action hiding behind the word 'opinion' on their compromised ratings.

When asked how they could miss the deteriorating credit quality of the bonds of Amtek and others, when the papers were reporting this regularly, their answer was frankly quite shocking: we have a periodic review and the quality drop did not show up as the review was still some months away! This attitude was worrisome because bond ratings, and therefore debt fund Risk-o-Meter, will have no meaning if the ratings don't reflect the bond quality on an ongoing basis correctly. SEBI then, possibly in a global first, got the rating agencies in India to stand behind their ratings and the changes in bond quality had to be mapped much better.[2]

With the debate about how to make debt funds and rating agencies mark risk better came the 2020 Franklin Templeton debt fund crisis. In April 2020, the fund house froze both entry and exit from six of its debt funds since it was facing large redemption pressures that went beyond the money the fund house had even after borrowing. The problem in this case was one of liquidity and not a credit downgrade. Lower rated bonds have a very thin secondary market in India and the fund house could not find buyers to sell the bonds to meet redemptions.

The lessons of the past five years went into the creation of a dynamic Risk-o-Meter that considers the various metrics of risk within an asset class and also captures the quality of the bond portfolio over the lifetime of the scheme. Therefore, SEBI needed a Risk-o-Meter that would not only capture the various risk metrics within debt funds (liquidity, interest rate and credit quality) but would also be dynamic to give a useful handle to the retail investor. The idea was that all this should be under the bonnet—the investor should not need to figure out the latest bond portfolio—that ask is too much. The only solution is to make the funds themselves responsible for an ongoing evaluation of the bond portfolio and then matching it to the risk categories.

All these market experiences, flaws and learnings went into the new Risk-o-Meter that SEBI made mandatory from 1 January 2021. There were four major changes that were made.

One, the number or risk categories increased to six: low, low to moderate, moderate, moderately high, high and very high risk. Risk level 1 was low and risk level 6 was very high. Overseas funds were marked risk level 7—it was off the charts on the risk metrics.

Two, the mapping of the risk levels with the portfolios was done not on category basis but on the basis of the actual portfolio at the time of the NFO. SEBI asked fund houses to use the formulas it gave to evaluate risk in debt portfolios on metrics of liquidity risk, interest rate risk and credit risk. Equity portfolios were to be evaluated on market cap, volatility and liquidity.

Three, the fund houses have to evaluate the portfolio risk at the end of every month and upload the risk rating on the AMFI site.[3]

Four, fund houses have to count the number of times in a year the risk metric changes. Investors and advisors now have a better handle to check if the risk in the scheme they have is bounding around from low to high and then decide whether to stay in the scheme or not. This is very important in debt funds since the portfolio quality can change dramatically over time. Investors should look for no changes in the Risk-o-Meter, especially in short-term debt funds.

Is the new Risk-o-Meter effective? Analyst firm Value Research did a comparison of the six Franklin Templeton debt schemes that were in trouble in 2020 and used the old Risk-o-Meter and the new one to evaluate the debt portfolios at the time of the incident.[4] The way the Risk-o-Meter is mapping risk is shown in Table 7.1.

Table 7.1

Risk profile of Franklin's closed funds		
The new Risk-o-Meter would have done a better job at identifying the risk inherent in Franklin's six shuttered debt funds		
Category	New Risk-o-Meter	Old Risk-o-Meter
Credit risk	Very high	Moderate
Dynamic bond	High	Moderate
Low duration	Moderately high	Moderate
Medium duration	Very high	Moderate
Short duration	Very high	Moderate
Ultra-short duration	Moderately high	Moderate

Source: Value Research

If investors had access to the new Risk-o-Meter earlier, they might not have bought into these debt funds thinking they are just moderately risky rather than being very high on the risk metric.

Using the Risk-o-Meter

All equity schemes are marked as high risk and very high risk. Investors understand that this is a risky asset class. The real value of the Risk-o-Meter is in evaluating debt funds. Counterintuitively, debt funds can be riskier than equity funds in some cases. Evaluating risk is very difficult for a retail investor or even advisors—this is something credit rating agencies and bond fund research desks might do well. But what you can do is look for Risk-o-Meter reading for the shortlisted schemes in your debt portfolio. Choose low risk in debt. Do not make the error of bringing home the risk into the debt part of your portfolio. Do not shoot for the highest return in debt. Stay with a low risk rating of 1 and 2. Check the risk rating at least four times in a year so that you don't get a shock. Have the link to the page on AMFI or your fund house that displays the Risk-o-Meter handy so that every few months you don't have to search for this.

But the chances of a repeat of the excesses of 2015–20 are low because SEBI has also made the categories truer to label than before. The chances of funds stuffing longer maturity funds in the low maturity category are now much lower. So, both the Risk-o-Meter and the new categorization make debt funds a much safer option than they were before.

Remember that fund houses will find ways to spot a loophole and stuff higher risk paper or strategies just to show higher returns to attract investors. If there is a big outlier in terms of returns in a particular category, be sure to examine its risk metrics very carefully.

One last thing you can do to manage the risk in your portfolio. Link the risk metric to your holding period. Any money you need within three years must have a low or low to moderate risk reading on the Risk-o-Meter. Medium-term money that you need between three to seven years must have low to moderate or moderate risk. Holding periods of more than seven years you go from moderately high to very high risk. The longer the holding period, the more risk you can take; the closer to today the need for money, lower is the risk.

Risk is not something you can avoid, so it is best to make friends with it and accept a reasonable risk approach rather than go blindly into negative real return products that do not give your money the growth over time that it needs to keep you funded in your later years. We are living longer and longer—we'll need our retirement pots to be large and inflation proof.

The next stop is at the tax station. Not something we like to give, but taxes cannot be avoided. There are asset classes and options that reduce your tax impact. So, let's get to it.

There is no investment that is risk free, the face of risk can be inflation, volatility, cost or illiquidity. Debt funds are sometimes riskier than equity index funds. Not pure return, good investment is about finding schemes with good risk-adjusted returns.

You are doing okay if you understand that

1. debt funds are not risk free;
2. the longer the tenor of the debt fund, the higher will be its risk level;
3. equity funds across categories will have different risk levels;
4. a small-cap fund will have much higher risk than a large-cap fund;
5. an index fund on Sensex or Nifty 50 is one of the least risky ways to build long-term wealth; and
6. SEBI's new Risk-o-Meter is very useful to judge the ongoing risk of debt funds.

8

TAXES

The joy of tax-paid wealth is the ability to sleep peacefully at night, to look yourself and your children in the eye.

I was in Hamburg over the summer of 2022 on a fellowship and found the waterfront along the warehouse district a compelling place to visit and wander around. Now a home to museums, clubs, bars and restaurants, the warehouses came up at the end of the nineteenth century as a duty-free zone in one of Europe's biggest ports—Hamburg—when the city joined the German Union. The tax-free status ensured the clustering of businesses related to global trade in that narrow stretch of land along the Elbe river that feeds into the North Sea. The warehouses fell into disuse as the tax-free status went away in 2013 and containerization took over from warehouses.

Many years ago, when in Singapore, I saw babies everywhere I looked. From newborns to toddlers, they were omnipresent. Prams everywhere. On asking around, I found that the government saw the population declining and gave tax incentives to couples to have babies!

These stories are not to tell you my tourist itinerary, but to bring home the point that taxes modify behaviour and smart governments use them to channel citizen actions into desired directions. All investments we make will have a tax consequence on the income and profit we earn from them. The government also incentivizes us to make investments in some products that are given a special tax status to bring down the total amount of tax we pay.

We go through various stages in our relationship with taxes that begin with 'I don't earn enough to care' to 'let's get this over with' each year and 'rage rage rage' at having to pay taxes. We need to accept that we have to pay taxes on income, spends and fruits of investments. There are more than sixteen countries in the world where there is no tax. In some you need to be born a citizen, in some you can buy citizenship and others are just unpleasant places to live. Other than these places, wherever you go, there are taxes. You have to pay taxes till you die (even after you retire, there are taxes) and they can chase the inheritors of your wealth in some cases.

Emotions of denial, hatred and rage against taxes need to be dealt with as early as possible. You cannot escape them without stepping out of the law. It helps to know why governments collect taxes. Governments need to spend on services such as defence, police, healthcare, education and so on. They need money for subsidies to sectors like agriculture and for the poor. And they need taxes to build infrastructure—both physical and digital. We can debate the quality of the services, but the fact that they are needed and therefore have to be funded is irrefutable.

How does the government get money to spend? Both from tax and non-tax revenue. Taxes take care of about 80 per cent of the total revenue of the government and the rest is the non-tax revenue. Non-tax revenue comes from dividends of public sector units, sale of government-owned businesses, sale of licenses like in telecom. Governments typically spend more than they get as revenue, and therefore need to borrow to fill the deficit. Total government expenditure is tax and non-tax revenue plus borrowing, also called deficit financing. A very large and sustained deficit has bad consequences (inflation, debt trap and could affect a country's overall global ratings making borrowing more and more expensive) for the economy and people; therefore, governments have ongoing pressure from economists to keep it under check.

Direct and indirect taxes

Taxes are both direct and indirect. Direct taxes are levied on your income and profit and indirect taxes are levied on your spending. Any form of income—salary, fees, rent, interest, dividend, royalty—is a candidate for a direct income tax. Any form of profit—from real estate, stocks, bonds, trading, gold, mutual funds (that invest in stocks, bonds, gold and real estate)—is a candidate for a direct tax. Direct taxes are called fair because they are usually progressive, which means that you pay a higher rate as your income increases.

The impact is more on a rich person than on a poor person. While the rates keep changing, India has three basic levels of income tax—5 per cent, 20 per cent and 30 per cent. As the income slabs rise, the rate of tax goes up. The government goes on tinkering with this, so it is best you check the latest slabs and tax rates on the government tax website.

But nothing in tax is simple. The effective rates change due to the impact of cess and surcharge. The Union government levies a cess to fund specific goals. For example, as of FY2023–24, there is a 4 per cent education and health cess that sits on top of the income tax rate, making the effective rates higher for everybody. To ensure that the rich pay a higher tax, those who earn above Rs 50 lakh of income in a year pay an additional surcharge on the tax they pay. The surcharge rate begins at 10 per cent and goes up to a huge 37 per cent under the old tax regime for those who earn an annual income above Rs 5 crore making the effective rate 42.7 per cent of income tax. These rates keep changing, so you need to look at the website of the tax department for the latest rates and information.[1]

Profits are called capital gain in tax language. Capital gain is the difference between your buying price and selling price. When the selling price is higher than the buying price, you have a capital gain. This can be short and long term, depending on the time difference between the buying and selling date. Short-term rates are usually higher than long-term rates, and in most cases treated like income. What is short and long term in the context of a holding period also differs across real estate, gold, stocks and bonds. It is very complicated for the average person to figure all this out, but it is important that you know the logic of the tax system so that you can plan your investments better.

Indirect taxes are levied on goods and services that you buy and are said to be unfair because the impact is the same on anybody who buys a good or service. A very rich person buying a car and a middle-class person buying a car will have the same rate of goods and services tax (GST) they pay. The GST is the goods and service tax regime that has collapsed all the various indirect taxes into one system. To make GST fairer, the rates differ according to who consumes the good or service. For example, there is zero GST on fresh fruits and vegetables. Branded rice, spices and edible oil carry a GST rate of 5 per cent. Items like contact lenses and specs pay 12 per cent.

Chocolates and ice cream have an 18 per cent rate. Luxury items such as ACs, cars, fizzy drinks pay a huge 28 per cent GST.[2] Alcohol and petroleum products are out of the purview of GST and are taxed separately.

Income tax basics

In India, income tax is calculated by incomes that arise under five heads. Income from salary, from house property, business and professional income, from other sources and from capital gain.

All the streams of income are added to give a gross total income number. From this the exempt income, or income that does not have any tax on it is removed. For example, agricultural income, gratuity and provident fund is exempt from income tax. Next, you use the various deductions to reduce the income that is offered for taxation to arrive at the total taxable income. You are then taxed at slab level. There is a rebate of the lowest slab. For those whose total taxable income is Rs 5 lakh or less, they get a rebate such that they pay no income tax. But those with the taxable income higher than Rs 5 lakh will continue to pay at the slab level in the old tax scheme. The new tax scheme with no deductions has a higher threshold.

Too tough? Tax is not easy. Try and understand or skip ahead and come back when you have a doubt while doing your annual tax return.

Notice that exemptions, deductions and rebates are three different ways to reduce your total tax paid. Do not confuse the three.

How to reduce the tax burden

Other than shifting to a country that has zero or low taxes, you need to work with the Indian tax system. There has been a historical aversion to paying taxes and we must understand why. Our lived and experienced collective memory is of a nation that was enslaved and conquered for the past many centuries. Taxes have been a way to subjugate the local populations—whether it was a jazia or a lagaan.

The deep-rooted, almost violent reaction that we have to paying taxes must be seen in the context of it being an explicitly exploitative tool to not just gather money, but to exhibit power and control. Post-Independence, the regime of corruption took over and it was the foolish who paid taxes. The smart people found ways to stay out of the tax net.

There is a much bigger story in the policy space of how the overall systemic corruption has been tackled in the past decade, but it must be said that the use of technology and the mapping of PAN with Aadhaar is tightening the noose around habitual tax evaders. The journey is long and hard, but increasing formalization of the economy is making the cost of tax evasion higher and higher. This is not to say there is no graft—there is. But the cost of not paying taxes is rising over the benefit of paying them and being free from the threat of a tax notice or worse.

The desire to not pay tax, even if it means putting yourself and your money at risk, is a behaviour I see most often when friends and family get to the point of a real estate sale. A few years back, a close relative was putting his old house in Noida on the block. As we all know, there is a black money component to most real estate deals. Take a full cheque payment, I advised, and pay the tax. The worry was the long-term capital gains tax to my relative and the higher stamp duty to the buyer. Wait for a full white deal and then just pay your taxes. Invest the money in a mutual fund portfolio and just step back. The relative did not need the money for the next ten years, so he could think of a good mix of equity along with some debt. He used the Section 54 EC route (invest in specific bonds that turn the profit tax-free) to take care of a part of the profit, but paid tax on the rest. Very reluctantly, against the wishes of all his friends and the rest of the family, he went with my advice. The mutual fund portfolio recovered the tax paid in under two years. He now goes around telling other people to just pay the tax and not deal with cash! How do you deal with crores worth of cash? The pitfalls are too many and is it really worth the pain, risk and the need to get into yet another real estate deal with the cash? Short point: pay your taxes after having taken all the legal routes available to reduce the burden.

Small lecture over! Let's get back to how to reduce our tax burden. On the indirect side, you can maximize your consumption of the zero or low GST items—home food over eating out. On the income side, you can earn as much exempt income as possible. Agricultural income is exempt and so is income from a United Nation entity. But not everybody can either be a farmer or a privileged UN employee. What you can do is to be aware of all the exemptions (like standard deduction, which is a deduction that acts as an exemption—sorry, I did say that the tax rules are ...), deductions and rebates.

The most popular deduction is the one under Section 80C. Tax rules are codified under various sections and the 80th section, with subsection C, allows for a Rs 1.5 lakh deduction (as of April 2023) on your gross total income to reduce the income offered for tax. The one relevant to us here is the deduction called ELSS or equity linked saving scheme. There is a special category of mutual funds that get you this tax benefit. If you invest Rs 1.5 lakh in an ELSS scheme, your taxable income reduces by that amount. So, if your total income being offered for taxation (after the other exemptions and deductions) was Rs 25 lakh, it will now be Rs 23.5 lakh. At the 30 per cent tax bracket (effective tax rate is 31.2 per cent in FY24), this works out to a tax saving of Rs 46,800. An easy way to see the tax impact is to multiply the deduction amount with the marginal (highest) tax rate applicable to your income to see the savings.

There are several other investments and spends that also give you the same benefit as an ELSS.[3] ELSS funds have a three-year lock-in. This means you cannot redeem your funds before this time. It is good that you are forced to stay in the product because equity takes a while to show results. I looked at a ten-year return period and found that as on 6 April 2023, the lowest ten-year return on an ELSS scheme was almost 12 per cent and the highest was 21 per cent year on year for ten years. The average return was around 15 per cent. Chosen carefully, as we will learn in Chapter 10, we can target higher than average returns in this category. What does a 15 per cent return over ten years, year on year mean? Rs 1.5 lakh invested ten years ago is now worth Rs 6.06 lakh. Not bad, right?

In 2020, the government announced a new tax scheme where you can get lower rates if you let go of all deductions and rebates.[4] Most people do not find the lower rates attractive enough to switch. Tax rules change year on year, so keep visiting the government's tax site for the latest updates.

Lowering tax on income and profit on assets

Another way to reduce your taxes is to opt for investments that have a zero or low tax rate on both income and capital gains. A quick rundown of the basics one more time. Savings become investments when they pass through asset classes such as equity, debt, gold and real estate. These give income (rent, interest and dividend) and profit. We need to have a mix of assets that give us the required income and lump sums in the future when needed.

You really must understand the difference between the income that assets throw off and the profit you make. I was teaching a postgraduate class the basics of mutual funds and was very surprised to see just how many students (despite being very good and attentive in class) got this quiz question wrong. Most confused income with profit. Let's take each asset one at a time and work through what the tax on their income and profit is. But take note that this can change as the government changes the rules around taxation each budget.

Always good to double check the current rate from the income tax site.[5]

Real estate

Other than agricultural land, which under special circumstances has no capital gains tax, real estate rent and profits are taxed. Rent from real estate is added to your income and taxed at your highest slab rate. If your income was Rs 25 lakh a year and you added a rent of Rs 15 lakh to this, then your total income (ignoring all other deductions and expenses related issues), your taxable income becomes Rs 40 lakh. At Rs 25 lakh you were already in the 30 per cent tax bracket. The rent of Rs 15 lakh will also be taxed at the same rate. Should you breach the Rs 50 lakh taxable income limit, you will have to pay a surcharge as well.

The profits can be short and long term. Short term in real estate is defined as a holding period of two years. This used to be three years till 2018, but in a bid to give a boost to the real estate sector, it was reduced to two years. Confused policy step, I think, but this is not a policy book. We'll just be takers of what the government decides and keep our opinions tightly bottled for now!

Real estate short-term profits are taxed at slab rate, like rent. These get added to your income and are taxed at your highest slab rate. For most readers of this book, you are looking in FY24 of slab rates between 31.2 per cent to 42.7 per cent. Long-term profits are taxed at 20 per cent of the profit *with indexation*. New word! Indexation. Belt up for another session of understanding a new concept.

You must have heard stories of the family elders talking about buying some property for a few lakhs that are now worth a few crores. Lost in the story is the long holding period of twenty or thirty years that turns lakhs into crores. Of concern to them is the huge profit such a sale today will mean. Over a twenty-year period, Rs 50 lakh that has turned into Rs 2 crore means a profit of Rs 1.5 crore (other costs not being considered here). This would mean a huge tax outflow of Rs 30 lakh (according to the current tax rates). But the prices twenty years ago cannot be compared to prices today. Inflation has caused a part of this price rise. Therefore, we need a way to inflation-index the prices of the past to bring them to comparable levels to today before we tax the profit.

The government gives a way to do this by using a price indexation route. You take the price of the past and make it up to date by using an inflation index published by the government. For example, Rs 50 lakh of 2002 becomes Rs 1.5 crore after indexation, giving a profit of Rs 49 lakh, on which the tax is Rs 9.8 lakh.

The formula you need to use is this:

> Indexed purchase price = Price of buying × (Index in year of sale/Index in year of purchase)[6]

For this example, the values are:

> Indexed price purchase = 50,00,000 × (317/105)
> = 1,50,95,238

If you don't want to pay even this tax, there are two other ways to go zero tax in a long-term real estate deal. Under Section 54 of the Income Tax Act, you can get an 'exemption' from this tax through two routes. One, if you have sold your residential property, then buying another residential property with the profit will get you an exemption from the long-term capital gains tax. You must buy this new property either one year before the sale or within two years of the sale to get this benefit.[7]

Another route is to buy bonds that are described in Section 54EC of the act. These are now called Section 54EC bonds. Bonds issued by Rural Electrification Corporation Limited, National Highway Authority of India, Power Finance Corporation Limited and Indian Railway Finance Corporation Limited give you this benefit. If you invest the profit (limited to Rs 50 lakh in a year) in any of these bonds within six months of the sale of the property, your profit is tax free. The lock-in is five years right now, but can change. These are low-interest-bearing bonds, and the interest you get is taxable at your slab rate. But when the principal returns to you, it is tax free.

The special case of REITs

Physical real estate is a difficult clunky asset that costs a lot both in terms of time and money when buying, while holding and at the time of sale. For investors who want an exposure to real estate without the accompanying problems, a mutual fund that invests in real estate can be an efficient option. A real estate investment trust (REIT) is a mutual fund–like product that invests in real estate, after raising funds from investors. Investors get back a mix of rent, dividend and profit that reflects in the NAV.

The product has been slow to take off in the Indian market due to a variety of historical issues that make investing in real estate difficult in India. The offerings at the moment are only the commercial real estate part of the market, though in countries like the United Kingdom, REITs are doing all kinds of products including malls, student housing and retirement homes.

Investors should manage their expectations when they invest in REITs. Debt plus returns and not equity returns is where you peg your return expectations. Anything over that is a bonus. REIT taxation is a bit different than that of physical real estate. Rent, interest and dividend are taxed at slab rate. The product goes long term at three years. Short-term capital gain is taxed at 15 per cent and long term at 10 per cent, after a tax-free profit of Rs 1 lakh.

Gold

The most-favoured traditional store of value and investment destination, gold is now available physically, as bonds and as a mutual fund product—both ETFs and index funds. Gold is a rare asset that throws off no income—interest, rent or dividend. It only gives a profit or a loss as the price goes up and down. The only exception is the sovereign gold bond that gives a small rate of interest.

Physical gold and gold funds go long term at three years. The short-term capital gains tax is deducted at slab rate for both physical gold and gold ETFs and index funds. Long-term capital gain is 20 per cent of profit with indexation. Budget 2024 has changed the indexation rules around some categories of funds, so please check for the latest rules.

Sovereign gold bonds' interest is taxed at slab rate and these go tax free on long-term capital gains after eight years. There is some confusion on whether this is five years or eight years and the answer is not clear as the tax department is yet to clarify this. Safer to take eight years as the duration of holding for these bonds in your investment calculations.

Debt

Under the large head of debt come all the fixed-income and related products such as fixed deposits, provident fund, public provident fund, all of the small saving products from the government, bonds, debt funds and all fund of funds. For some reason, the tax department is unwilling to consider equity-based fund of funds as equity for the tax treatment. So even the equity fund of funds that invest overseas in pure equity products are taxed as debt!

Fixed deposits are not tradeable therefore carry no capital gains, and no tax on profit. This and other deposit interest is taxable at slab level. Then, PF and PPF are unique products in India that give an EEE tax benefit to you. These are exempt from tax on investment as they carry the Section 80C benefit. The interest they earn over the holding period is exempt from tax. At withdrawal, there is no tax either. So, PF and PPF are powerful products to build the core of the debt part of your portfolio. More of this in Chapter 12 as we construct portfolios.

If you opt for the income distribution cum capital withdrawal—the IDCW (check page 88 in Chapter 5 to remember what these are) option in debt funds—it gets added to your income and you get taxed at slab rate. Dividends were tax free in the hands of investors till FY20, but now get added to income and the tax is paid by the investor directly.

Earlier than FY2023–24, bonds and debt funds would go long term at three years. The short-term capital gain was taxed at slab rate and the long-term rate was 20 per cent with indexation. But a last-minute insertion into the Finance Bill in end March 2023 killed this tax advantage for debt funds and took away the distinction between short- and long-term and indexation benefit. Debt funds are now taxed similar to fixed deposits. But again, tax rules change often and check the latest rules at the time of your reading this book.

Equity

Similar to debt funds, if you have chosen the IDCW option, the money that comes into your account from the income of the fund gets added to your income and is taxed at slab rate. Equity funds go long term at just one year. Short-term capital gains are taxed at 15 per cent and the long-term rate, after a profit of Rs 1 lakh a year has been taken, is 10 per cent. The long-term capital gains tax on equity was introduced in FY2019 at a nominal 10 per cent, removing the unique tax-free status that the asset class enjoyed for many years. The equity rates might change as well. Like I said, keep updating this information before you take a decision based on the tax impact of an investment.

IDCW or growth option?

The various tax rules make it important to choose your exit choices carefully when investing in mutual funds. In Chapter 5 we came across two choices offered on how the money grows in a mutual fund. The growth option does not return any money to you till you redeem and the IDCW option gives you a periodic burst of income depending on when the mutual fund declares a dividend.

Dividends, we know, get added to your income and are taxed at slab rate. For most people reading this book, this would be a 30 per cent tax rate. The growth option tax impact will differ across debt and equity products. Debt profits, from FY2023–24, get added to income and the impact is the same as the divided option. Equity has an advantage since the long-term capital gains tax is just 10 per cent. In the current tax regime, the growth option scores over the IDCW option for equity.

But what if you need a regular income from your portfolio? Enters the option called SWP or a systematic withdrawal plan. While an IDCW option leaves you at the mercy of the fund house to declare a dividend, an SWP allows you to fix the amount of money you want to withdraw each month, quarter or any other periodicity that is allowed by the mutual fund. In both debt and equity, for slab rates of 20 per cent or more, the growth option works out better even in an SWP. You need to be careful about exit loads and holding periods to not trigger higher costs before you go in for an SWP.

The tax rates, rules and regimes keep changing year on year. The way to use this chapter is to understand the tax system. Understand that incomes and profits are taxed at different rates. Profits can be short or long term. This chapter is intended to give you a very broad overview of the applicable tax rules. For each rate mentioned above, there will be fine print and details that usually your chartered accountant will be able to describe better. Anyhow, bigger and better things lie ahead, like how to create a portfolio and finally, how to choose a mutual fund scheme. But first, let's reduce the choice set. Let's go.

Your choices at the point of entry will result in you paying higher or lower taxes on exit. A basic understanding of the Indian tax system is essential as you will be paying taxes over your entire lifetime.

You are doing okay if you understand that

1. income from an asset is not the same as profit;
2. rent, interest, dividend is called income from an asset;
3. profit can be short or long term;
4. income is usually taxed at slab level;
5. short- and long-term profit tax rates vary according to asset class; and
6. an SWP is more tax efficient than an income-distribution option.

9

REDUCING CHOICE

Choosing is easier and satisfaction levels higher if you reduce the universe of choices out there.

After the first euphoria of getting your paperwork in place, making a plan, deciding your goals and putting down savings target for each month is over, the hard task of actually choosing asset classes and products begins. If the architect's drawing and modelling tells you what the final building looks like, unless the contractor and the labour get their hands into the bricks and cement, nothing will happen and your mahal will remain in the hawa. Castles in the air look so wonderful in our imagination, but each piece that goes into the actual thing needs to be chosen, bought and then used. The first part was both tough and easy—it was tough to begin the process of asset consolidation, getting bank accounts in place and figuring out goals. But that was also the easy part since no decision had to be taken to actually put the money down just yet.

It is once you enter the marketplace that it really hits you. The sense of being overwhelmed and frozen is real. Even people like me, who have been so closely associated with finance, feel the total blanking out when it comes to deciding on what to buy. I remember once I was in the market for a liquid fund many years ago. The new SEBI rules that (in 2020) make choice much easier were not in place. I remember doing five screen downs on my desktop, scrolling down names, versions, options (daily, weekly, monthly dividend, growth, dividend reinvestment) and hastily shutting the site. The overwhelmed feeling was physical. I called up a colleague (we still call him Dr Fund, but his real name is Kayezad E. Adajania!) who knows mutual funds better than they know themselves and just asked for a name.

Instead of trying to choose between products, it is always better to begin with your own money needs that have to be addressed. It is better to narrow down the options rather than stare at the universe of choice available. I remember, on one of my earlier trips to the UK as a student, entering a supermarket, staring at the wall of coffee, with literally hundreds of options, trying to not look broken as women around me confidently grabbed their bottles and clickety-clacked away on those heels—I mean how do they even stand in something that high and that thin! But I need to quickly get back to funds before I pull this thread any further and get into some serious trouble with the feminists. I began to then whittle down my option set—it was easier to make a I-don't-want list first. I don't want decaf. I don't want anything that costs more than xyz, I don't want exotic filters, or coffee that has passed through the intestine of a civet (don't even get me started on this one). In my twenties, with very little money or taste, I just wanted some cheap instant coffee. With that in mind, it was much easier to narrow down the choice set to three or four and then just experiment with the various brands till I got what I liked.

Our money lives are no different. There are choices between asset classes (equity, debt, real estate, gold) that we need to make and then within asset classes there are products we need to choose (FD, PPF, bonds, bond funds under the debt allocation, for example) and then within some of these categories, there are further choices. The overwhelmed feeling continues even after you choose mutual funds. There are thirty-seven categories for just open-ended funds.

Each fund house has one scheme per category. But categories like index funds already have more than 180 schemes within it. Close-ended funds through target maturity funds ,are a fast-rising category of funds as well. There are over 1200 schemes already in the market. Each scheme has options—growth and income distribution (IDCW), regular or direct, through SIP or lump sum. All the permutations and combinations make for a frozen first-time investor. Heck, even an old investor like me is continuously stumped as the choice set just goes on expanding.

We need a way to reduce the choice set in front of us. A filter is needed to reduce the sheer volume of choice we face. We need to begin taking very basic but existential decisions right away.

Choosing categories

As I rushed to complete the deadline for this book, I worked already weak neck muscles too much and spent the last three weeks of 2022 in physiotherapy—not the Tihar jail Satyendar Jain kind, but the real one. One of the doctors there googled me and brought me her portfolio pain points. For a person who does not understand markets or balance sheets, but is smart enough to help people recover from injuries and pain, she was making very basic money mistakes. Her portfolio had funds from high-risk mutual fund sectors such as technology and small-cap.

She had IPOs in her portfolio. She was in direct stocks. And she was stressing that she had lost money in all of them. *Abhi to minus chal raha hai, ek saal ho gaya.*

I go into total maun (silence) when I see such portfolio errors. This is the pain of seeing tax-paid money go into products that might not be the best starting points for a market-linked investment portfolio. Of not understanding that equity needs at least an investing horizon of seven to ten years before you see results. Her portfolio was based on tips and media hype about some stocks, IPOs and funds. It had no relationship with what she needed and what was suitable for her age, stage, knowledge level and needs. What if a person comes with a leg injury, I asked her, do you get to right away asking him to run a 100-metre race? Or does he slowly get the muscle strength back before he begins to walk normally? Running is a long way off. Why are you investing in things you know nothing about?

Just as you are building my neck muscles, you need to build your financial literacy quotient before you get into risk-based products. Of course, she's now reading *Let's Talk Money* as a starting point to her sensible investment journey. What should she have done differently? Understood that there are different categories of mutual funds and each of the thirty-seven categories can be matched to an investor profile and the financial problem that the investor wants solved.

We need to begin this journey by removing the categories that are of no use to an average retail portfolio. I said earlier that some categories were allowed as a negotiation with the industry. The mutual fund industry's point was this: if several thousand crores worth of money finds the category good enough to invest in, why will the regulator take that category away?

Before we can choose the categories, we need to revisit the three boxes in your money box that we created in *Let's Talk Money* in Chapter 10. The Almost There box has financial products that are needed for very short-term use—between tomorrow and three years. The In Some Time box has financial products you need for money needs that are between three-to-seven years away. And the Far Away box has products that will give the needed money after seven years at least. We use the distance from today to shortlist products and not the return they give. The closer to today the money need, the lower will be the return and we should be okay with it.

Almost There box

The Almost There box needs financial products that you will use to give you the money you need within three years. The needs can be tomorrow, next month, in six months, in a year or two or three—whatever your particular situation is. This box is easier to estimate than the others since we have a better handle of what is just ahead of us than what is far away.

What is the most important attribute of a driver or a cab? That he shows up on time. The car needs to be there when you have to leave for your meeting, airport or office. The money that you need in the next three years must be there when you need it. You cannot have a downturn in the stock market at a time when the fees for your course abroad need to be paid or when the down payment of the house is due. This money cannot be subject to the risk of the principal losing value (as is possible in real estate, gold, traded bonds and stocks). The money you need tomorrow needs to be in your bank account, ready for transfer.

The other attribute is that the money should be liquid. You cannot go to market with a property and assume that the money will be with you in a month. Real estate is an illiquid asset. Similarly, if you have a long-term close-ended product such as an endowment policy or a pension product, you cannot bank on them to give you the money needed. It cannot be stocks since markets go up and down.

For money needs that are immediate, you need your savings deposit (or current account if you use one) to have the money to spend. For needs within three years, the risk-free product you can use is a fixed deposit with a large commercial bank (not cooperative, not corporate deposits). We all know this product and for money you don't mess with, it is still a go-to destination.

But do think of migrating to mutual funds, especially if you need the money in six months or more because of the liquidity and return advantage they bring. The asset class you use is debt. Never equity or gold. Within debt, which has sixteen categories, we can shortlist three.

The categories you need that are matched to your money needs across three years are liquid, money market and banking and PSU funds. See the categories matched to holding period in Table 9.1.

Table 9.1

Short-term investment objective	
Holding period	Category
Three months or less	Liquid
Within two years	Money market
After two years	Banking and PSU

Remember two things when you plan for money needs within three years. One, do not go for the highest return you can get even within debt funds. Two, don't stress too much in trying to maximize your return by a too-tight mapping of needs with fund categories. Life is not neat and the money need that is six months away might get pushed to eight months.

And what is twelve months away will be three months away in nine months. So, if you have a money market fund for the goal that is one year away, you will need to move it to a liquid fund in nine months. Extend this exercise to five or six short-term needs and the cost of time and attention to this becomes very large.

What to do?

Use simple routes to managing money rather than trying to match your needs to every debt category available. This approach might not maximize returns, but makes for a time-, cost- and attention-efficient one. Use the liquid fund category as a very short-term deposit and redeem a week before you need the money and have it ready for use in your bank account. Be very risk averse when it comes to money needs that are immediate.

Instead of tightly matching money needs to the other categories that go from three months to three years, use the money market funds to park money that you will need within the next two years. As the time for withdrawal comes nearer, redeem at least a month in advance from this category as well.

Next, use banking and PSU bond funds for needs that are two years or more away, but do remember to check the average maturity of the scheme you select as this varies quite a bit over the schemes in the category. The average maturity of the schemes should match your holding-period requirement. A wrong matching of your holding period with the maturity dates of the bonds in the scheme might end up badly for you.

Another set of funds that are very useful to target a lump sum in the future are target maturity funds (TMF). These are index funds with a portfolio of bonds that mature on a particular date. For very specific goals, TMF are good to use with the maturity date matching your need. But there are problems with this category. While you will get a list of funds that are opening on the AMFI site[1] and on the Value Research site[2], nowhere will you be told the indicative return because SEBI does not allow it. So, unless you are working with an advisor or a distributor or your bank is friendly, you won't get the indicative yield of these funds. The indicative yields are usually verbally told to distributors and financial advisors or sit in fund house PowerPoint presentations that are shared in closed loops.

There is a lot of innovation going on in this category, so do keep updating yourself to see if this set of funds becomes useful at a later date than when this book was written.

In Some Time box

This is money you need between three and seven years. This could be a down payment of a house, money for your own marriage or that of your child, money for your further education or for a child—different ages and stages will need money for a variety of things in the middle distance of your life. To put an exact date is difficult, to put an exact amount is difficult, so work with approximations. Overestimate what you will need and underestimate the distance from today. The categories I like to work with for this time period are in Table 9.2.

Table 9.2

Medium-term investment objective	
Holding period	Category
Three to seven years	Banking and PSU
Five to seven years	Conservative hybrid

I will take some risk with money I need in this box, but not too much. The further away from today the need is, the more risk I can take. There can be many strategies to target your returns for this time band and I use a simple two-category route. I use a mix of banking and PSU and conservative hybrid.

Why not the others? The duration-based funds have seen a much tighter regulatory regime post 2019 and I would like to wait till we have seen a seven- to ten-year period before I begin to use them. Corporate bonds are an option but the credit downgrade is a worry, especially after the adventures of the past few years in this category as well. Well-chosen banking and PSU funds give you a lower risk way to get a higher return compared to a fixed deposit. As you move beyond five years to goal time frame, begin using the conservative hybrid category.

Then, TMF is a great new addition to a lower risk way to get money for a definite goal in the future, but it will suffer from the lack of a published indicative yield. But keep watching the category for more innovation and they might be the solution to target-specific goals at a specific time for a tiny cost.

There will be many other ways to hold money for short- and medium-term needs in debt funds. I have tried to keep it very simple rather than have a very rigid focus on meeting needs with the exactly right category. For many categories, such as floating rate funds, corporate bond and credit risk funds, it is best that you work with an advisor or good distributor who can tell you which one suits your exact need. Debt can be a higher risk ride simply because of the nearness of the goal to today. I will choose a very low-risk ride rather than make an error in choosing a potentially higher risk route.

Far Away box

Counterintuitively, once defined, I find the far away goals much easier to work towards than those that are closer to today using mutual funds! I am not a big fan of debt funds for money needs more than seven years away. Of course, your long-term debt portfolio should have PPF and PF (if you are eligible) as the core.

Of the eleven equity categories and the six hybrid categories, the ones mentioned in Table 9.3 are relevant to an average investor.

Table 9.3

Long-term investment objective	
Holding period	Category
More than seven years	Broadmarket equity index
More than seven years	Large- and mid-cap
More than seven years	Mid-cap
More than seven years	Small-cap
More than seven years	Multi-cap
More than seven years	ELSS
More than seven years	Foreign

I have kept large-cap funds out because it is getting increasingly difficult for them to beat the benchmarks. In repeated studies it is found that most large-cap funds underperform the benchmarks. You are better off in a low-cost index fund. You remove the fund manager risk along with the need to monitor a big chunk of your equity portfolio. The large- and mid-cap category gives a minimum 35 per cent allocation to mid- and large-caps each, with the rest usually in large-caps, allowing fund managers to show some outperformance.

I have kept out dividend yield, value/contra as they do not have any special edge to the categories included here. Focused funds are difficult to place because they can be across any market cap. These are better used by advisors and distributors who can find individual portfolio gaps to fill with these funds if needed. Flexi-cap as a category leaves the allocation between the three market caps to the discretion of the fund manager. Most flexi-cap funds seem to have a large-cap bias. A better way to get a multi-cap exposure is the multi-cap category that mandates a minimum exposure to each cap. Sectoral/thematic are high-risk categories that cannot be recommended in a book. These don't work for everybody. If you have a deep insight into a sector—maybe you work in pharma or IT or FMCG—and therefore you have a view on the sector and its prospects, you can add that to your portfolio. But as a category for generic use, I cannot include it here.

The ELSS funds are a great option to get the Section 80C tax deduction and have your money earn a good return. This is for people who do not exhaust their limits with PF and PPF. Foreign funds are very high risk and only for mature mutual fund investors with a portfolio size that is large enough to need them for further diversification. These are not a part of a starter portfolio of mutual funds.

We now have a shortlist of the fund categories. We now have twelve categories, with equity taking up seven of these. I have kept the choice very small in the debt categories due to the difficulty of retail investors dealing with a debt portfolio. It is far more dynamic than equity and active funds need a very frequent oversight.

In the next chapter, we will begin using these categories to select funds. And in Chapter 12, we will build some basic portfolios using these categories. I will not recommend fund names, but leave you with tools to do that. This is the chapter you have been waiting for. Let's get to it.

We freeze with too much choice and delay decisions. But if we do choose from too many options rather than a smaller set, our satisfaction levels are lower. We need a system to reduce the sheer volume of choice available in the Indian mutual fund market.

You are doing okay if you understand that

1. it is best to stay with a manageable set of choices when shortlisting categories;
2. you need a mix of liquid, money market and banking and PSU bond funds for short-term needs;
3. you need a mix of banking and PSU bond fund and conservative hybrid funds for medium-term needs;
4. you need a mix of index, large- and mid-cap, multi-cap, ELSS, mid-cap, small-cap and foreign funds for long-term investing;
5. there may be many other shortlists possible, but there will never be a perfect one; and
6. perfect can be the enemy of good and works to stop you from taking decisions that might not be perfect.

10

CHOOSING SCHEMES

The hard work of the initial years looks a lot like luck (but isn't) when it bears fruit.

Have you seen a fifty-year-old woman select vegetables and fruit at the local market? Her total focus is on the right price and quality. The produce is prodded and poked gently. The colour, texture and shape examined carefully. The freshness confirmed by sometimes digging a nail into the veggie surface. All the while telling the vendor how poor the stuff is, the final aim being a reduction of price. She did not begin this way. As a young girl, she would bring home whatever the vendor gave her. She had no idea how to choose. But years of running her own home and figuring out by trial and error, she has become an expert on getting the best out there for what she thinks is the best price.

Choosing schemes is a bit like that. You don't go to the marketplace and buy whatever tip you have received or whichever fund looks shiny and nice. There is an art and a science to selecting funds for your unique portfolio. I will tell you the process I follow to select funds. There can be several other roads to do this. My road takes a lot of time at the point of selection. Hours and hours of work. But once the portfolio is selected and every scheme has fought for its place in my money box, I don't change it. I review it once a year. Schedule time with my husband and we make a nice event out of putting each scheme through the stern lens of performance, risk, cost and consistency. We look at the asset allocation and decide to sell or buy the winning or losing asset class. Decide which funds to sell and which to buy. This is the choice part. The execution will happen over weeks or months depending on the size of the amount to be moved.

Do we get the best return? I am sure we do not. Do we always have the top-performing scheme? Almost never. Do we worry about our portfolio? Almost never. Is there money when we want it? Always yes. The road we follow is one that allows the money to hum quietly in the background while we do the things we like to do. Money decisions happen once or twice a year. Not more than that. If you ask me the value of the market, most days I have no idea.

You will have your own unique roads to follow. What comes next is the process. It is not perfect, but it is good. My credo is: let perfect not be the enemy of the good! There is nothing that is perfect in life. There are moments that approach perfection, but it is not a continuous state. Understanding this about life and about your mutual fund portfolio will release you from performance pressure and therefore not taking action at all.

Shortlisting schemes

Shortlisting a maximum of six to ten funds from the thousands out there is an intimidating task. Even with reducing choice by filtering out the categories that are not useful, there is the pressure to pick schemes from within the categories that you can trust your money to.

The funds have to jump through the hoops of good performance, low risk, low cost and consistency. To do a deep-dive in data and look through the innards of the scheme is not something most investors can do. I suggest a simpler route. There are at least three credible mutual fund data firms in India that also put out league tables, performance measures, risk statistics, portfolio details and a whole truckload of other data. I will use these as a starting point to make the task easier.

There are three rankings that have a defined process of giving star ratings and rankings to schemes: Value Research, Morningstar and CRISIL.[1,2,3]

I find Value Research the easiest to use with a far better understanding of what an average investor might need in order to go deeper behind the star ratings. It is also a good idea to select schemes from one rating and then see how many of these feature in the other two as well.

Steps for shortlisting funds

First, choose the category that you want to populate with one or two schemes. Let's pick large- and mid-cap as the category we want to work on. Let's assume that you have chosen this category as part of your ten-year-plus goal. But there are more than twenty-five schemes in this category and we need only one.

Second, look at the star ratings and rankings. Most of them already use risk-adjusted return (see page 147 in Chapter 7) as a filter to remove the riskier options from their top-rated schemes. We can begin with this and then build our own methodology. Choose not just the five-star rated, but also the four-star rated. Not just the top rank, but also rank two. Consistent funds go up and down the rankings and the fund manager might have a bad couple of years. Now, we have a long list to work on. In this category, this number will be around ten to twelve. This is a very manageable number to do further research as compared to twenty-five to thirty-four schemes that might be out there. Ideally, create an Excel sheet or have a sheet of paper where you take down the various schemes as rated and ranked by these different companies.

Look at Table 10.1 to see how it might look on your paper or worksheet.

Table 10.1

Category name: large- and mid-cap				
		Rating 1	Rating 2	Rating 3
1	Fund 1	✓	✓	✓
2	Fund 2	✓		
3	Fund 3		✓	✓
4	Fund 4	✓	✓	✓

Category name: large- and mid-cap				
		Rating 1	Rating 2	Rating 3
5	Fund 5	✓	✓	✓
6	Fund 6	✓		
7	Fund 7	✓		
8	Fund 8		✓	✓
9	Fund 9			✓
10	Fund 10	✓	✓	

Third, keep this information aside for the moment. We will come back to it once the entire process is done. Now we deep dive into using performance, consistency, risk and cost metrics to shortlist schemes. Choose one of the data sites that give you access to various metrics across fund houses, categories and schemes. I am using the data from Value Research, but there are plenty of data options and this is a space that will see an increasing number of offerings; so, update your choice if a better option comes along. Now begin with looking at performance data and go as far back as the data set you use allows.

In Table 10.2, I have shortlisted schemes with twenty-year performance histories. We don't get the direct option (go to page 84 in Chapter 5 to refresh what this means) data for this time period. So, I have gone with the regular option, just to see how the schemes might do on consistency over a very long period of time. This is real data, but I am anonymizing the scheme names and dates so that this does not become a recommendation. It is meant to trigger your own research—

there are enough 'top funds to invest' resources on the web and I will certainly not add to that noise!

Table 10.2

Twenty-year ranks and performance			
	Name	Rank	Return (%)
1	Fund 1	1/6	22.05
2	Fund 2	2/6	20.81
3	Fund 3	3/6	18.85
All regular funds			

This is real data of the six funds available with a twenty-year history, I am taking the top three as a shortlist. I am looking at schemes that make it to the top two quartiles. If there are 100 schemes, twenty-five at the top is the top quartile, the next twenty-five is the second quartile, the next twenty-five the third and the last twenty-five the fourth quartile. Next, we look at a fifteen-year return history in Table 10.3. We are still using the regular plan option for this time cut as well.

Table 10.3

Fifteen-year ranks and performance			
	Name	Rank	Return (%)
1	Fund 4	1/14	12.81
2	Fund 1	2/14	10.23
3	Fund 5	3/14	10.19
4	Fund 6	4/14	10.11

Fifteen-year ranks and performance			
	Name	Rank	Return (%)
5	Fund 2	5/14	9.52
6	Fund 7	6/14	9.22
7	Fund 8	7/14	9.20
All regular funds			

There are now fourteen schemes to choose from and I am taking the top seven that make up the first and second quartile. We see that Fund 1 and Fund 2 both show up on this list, but we lose Fund 3. Next, we look at ten-year returns in Table 10.4, and move to the direct plan from this time cut onwards.

Table 10.4

Ten-year ranks and performance			
	Name	Rank	Return (%)
1	Fund 9	1/15	22.28
2	Fund 4	2/15	20.32
3	Fund 1	3/15	16.65
4	Fund 10	4/15	16.21
5	Fund 11	5/15	16.09
6	Fund 8	6/15	15.82
7	Fund 2	7/15	15.67
8	Fund 12	8/15	15.33
9	Fund 5	9/15	15.08
All direct funds			

There are now fifteen funds and we look at the top nine. Fund 1 and Fund 2 show up here as well. Now we have Fund 4, 5 and 8 that see a repeat of the top two quartile performance over the fifteen-year period. See how the schemes are moving up and down as we change the time period. The top-ranked scheme of twenty years ago moves to rank 3 over a ten-year period. And Fund 3 is lost fully from the league tables. We now look at the five-year return data in Table 10.5.

Table 10.5

Five-year ranks and performance			
	Name	Rank	Return (%)
1	Fund 9	1/18	13.38
2	Fund 11	2/18	12.97
3	Fund 12	3/18	12.95
4	Fund 10	4/18	12.73
5	Fund 5	5/18	12.53
6	Fund 13	6/18	12.38
7	Fund 1	7/18	12.29
8	Fund 4	8/18	11.43
9	Fund 8	9/18	11.18
All direct funds			

There are now eighteen funds to choose from and we take the top nine. Fund 1 is still here, though we have lost Fund 2. Fund 4, 5 and 8 reappear. New candidates are fund 9, 10 11 and 12.

Do you see where I am going with this? Next, is the three-year ranking in Table 10.6.

Table 10.6

Three-year ranks and performance			
	Name	Rank	Return (%)
1	Fund 15	1/25	27.09
2	Fund 16	2/25	22.18
3	Fund 5	3/25	21.74
4	Fund 1	4/25	20.49
5	Fund 13	5/25	20.27
6	Fund 4	6/25	19.75
7	Fund 9	7/25	19.68
8	Fund 17	8/25	19.87
9	Fund 12	9/25	19.60
10	Fund 18	10/25	19.28
All direct funds			

There are now twenty-five schemes and we look at the top ten—we are beginning to drop the lower names on the second quartile as the number of schemes is rising. Do not look at three-year and one-year data to decide your schemes as some distributors would want you to do. But we must look at performance nearer to today to judge the continuation of performance history. We see Fund 1 still here. Hello again, Fund 1! Funds 4, 5 and 9 are continuing to hold their place.

Some names are already jumping out from this list of funds across years. But we are not choosing just yet. We are starting to notice such things. See that I am trying to map performance consistency over time. The highlighted schemes are in the top two quartiles most of the time. If any fund does not show up in at least three out of five time periods, I will remove it. Let's go through the list in Table 10.7.

Table 10.7

How to map consistency of performance	
Fund 1	Makes the cut across all time periods
Fund 2	Makes the cut in three out of five time periods
Fund 4	Makes the cut in four out of five time periods
Fund 5	Makes the cut in four out of five time periods
Fund 8	Makes the cut in three out of five time periods
Fund 9	Makes the cut in three out of five time periods
Fund 12	Makes the cut in three out of five time periods

We now have a shortlist of just seven funds to dive deeper to see risk and cost. We are trying to reduce the number of schemes at every step to end up with two or three of which we might choose one or two, depending on the size of the portfolio and the diversification needed. See that Fund 1 is there in all time periods, Funds 4 and 5 are there in four out of five time periods. These are huge plus points for these funds.

Fourth, examine the risk. I used the Fund Compare tool on Value Research to do this.[4] You should use whatever platform or tool set you find useful. I shortlist the seven funds and begin looking deeper into their insides. We need to see the risk metrics that were discussed in Chapter 7 and apply them to a real-life story. Look at page 153, Chapter 7 to see the risk attributes again.

The risk ratios have no meaning on their own. They need to be seen in relation to the metrics of the other shortlisted funds. Using this filter, let's look at how our candidates do on the filter of risk in Table 10.8, sorted on Alpha.

Table 10.8

Mapping the risk of the shortlisted funds								
Fund name	Fund risk grade	Fund return grade	Risk-o-Meter	Standard deviation	Sharpe ratio	Sortino ratio	Beta	Alpha
Fund 5	Average	Above average	Very high	24.14	0.80	0.88	1.02	4.15
Fund 4	Average	Above average	Very high	21.87	0.80	0.86	0.93	3.46
Fund 1	Below average	High	Very high	23.99	0.77	0.77	1.01	3.46
Fund 12	Low	Above average	Very high	21.56	0.77	0.86	0.93	2.74
Fund 9	Below average	High	Very high	22.59	0.77	0.84	0.98	2.69
Fund 2	Average	Average	Very high	23.37	0.65	0.68	1.00	0.16
Fund 8	Average	Below average	Very high	21.05	0.60	0.63	0.90	−0.77

Notice that the Risk-o-Meter risk grade is very high in each case. SEBI ranks all equity funds at very high, so this information has no meaning here. Most analyst firms will give their own evaluation of the risk and return grades.

These are good pointers to how much risk the scheme has taken to deliver the return. We are ranking the schemes in descending order sorting on Alpha—or the excess return over the benchmark. Fund 5 is showing high benchmark-plus returns, but its risk as measured by standard deviation is also the highest. It is doing good on the Sharpe and Sortino ratios, but Beta is more than 1.

Fund 4 is next on the high-Alpha list with a much lower standard deviation and doing well on other risk parameters. Fund 1 is our long-term performer which does well on Alpha, but not so well on standard deviation.

Table 10.8 highlights the risk attributes, but it can get very confusing for an average investor. I can tell you, it gets intimidating to me too. Alpha, Beta, Sortino—they are stuff out of nightmares. Supplement your analysis by looking at the risk and return grades that Value Research assigns to get a better picture of the risk taken and the return given. Funds 1 and 9 are showing below-average risk and high return. Funds 4, 5, 8 and 12 are showing average risk and above-average return.

Fifth, look at the cost. On the same tool we can see the expense ratios (see page 117 in Chapter 6) of our candidates. This is shown in Table 10.9.

Table 10.9

Expense ratio	
Fund name	Expense ratio (%)
Fund 5	1.11
Fund 1	1.05

Expense ratio	
Fund name	Expense ratio (%)
Fund 2	0.92
Fund 9	0.68
Fund 8	0.66
Fund 4	0.60
Fund 12	0.48

Fund 5 is charging 1.11 per cent and Fund 1 is charging 1.05 per cent on a direct plan. Fund 12 is charging less than half at 0.48 per cent. Expense ratios are very important, especially in years when the fund is underperforming the benchmark. While the returns are posted net of all costs, we must keep in mind a fund house that is charging substantially less. It shows honesty of intent.

Remember what we read in Chapter 6—the costs of fund management do not rise as the assets under management go up.

Considering all these factors and looking at long-range performance, the four funds that stand out are Fund 1, Fund 4, Fund 5 and Fund 9. This is not to say that the others are not investment worthy. Also, remember that performance and other metrics are constantly changing and our attempt is to pin down consistency over time of all the relevant factors. Fund 1 is looking good on parameters of consistency, returns, cost and risk. Finally, the choice between the four will also depend on how you perceive the fund house. These are all well-known names and you might prefer one AMC over another.

Check back to see if the shortlisted funds here are featuring in other league tables (step two earlier). This is just another validation that our process is correct. If the same set of schemes are filtering through various independent analyses, then it is reasonable to conclude that the shortlisted funds are indeed jumping through the hoops we have created here. Also check the one-year performance just to make sure the fund has not had a particularly bad year. If so, do a deeper check to see if there has been a change in the fund manager or in the fund house management. It could just be that the fund is having a bad year.

You can go deeper into the choice and begin looking at other metrics such as SIP returns and fund manager consistency. Whatever metric you choose, one of these seven will show up in different positions. The final choice comes down to what you value more. Does having a consistent performer outweigh a higher return metric in some years? Do lower costs give you a higher sense of confidence? Does the tenor of the fund manager over time gives you more comfort? You will have to answer some of these questions and then choose the scheme you want to invest in. There is no one right answer. You are looking for a scheme that you will not have to change for at least a decade. Look for a long-term consistent performer with reasonable risk and cost metrics.

Often, I hear people tell me: I am just unlucky. I begin investing and the fund performance does down. I would like to tell them: you are not that important in the scheme of things that your buying into a scheme will alter its performance history. Look for some other factor—of course, I don't say that to them, but I can say it here in the book! Remember that you are not unlucky. Luck plays a role when you time markets. If you do this much work and choose one scheme and it has a bad year, give it time to recover. A fund that has a ten-year performance history is not going to roll over and die just because there is one bad year.

Shorter term outperformers

There will be often a fund house that is new in the industry and pushes very hard to show performance, reduce costs and manage risk. If you notice some shorter term performers like that, select those to do a deep dive on risk metrics and cost. While this does not become your first choice, it can make the cut for a category diversifier. The risk of a fund house and scheme with less than five-year performance history is very high, so this approach is good only for the investor who has been with mutual funds for at least one down-market cycle.

For example, Fund 15 had a great three-year return metric and was ranked number one with super cost and risk metrics. But on one-year performance, it was ranked the lowest. It dropped from number one to number twenty-three between a three-year and a one-year ranking. That's why I reward consistency over the longest period of return available over most other metrics.

Debt funds

This is a far tougher category to pin down because the bond portfolio will change often in a shorter term scheme and the underlying bonds can lose credit quality over the time period of your holding the scheme. Let's do this exercise for money market funds. These are funds we use for money needs up to two years away from today. But we begin by looking at long-term performance, in Table 10.10, just to see consistency of returns over time.

Table 10.10

Ten-year ranks and performance			
	Name	Rank	Return (%)
1	Fund 1	1/12	7.52
2	Fund 2	2/12	7.43
3	Fund 3	3/12	7.43
4	Fund 4	4/12	7.35
5	Fund 5	5/12	7.27
6	Fund 6	6/12	7.25
All direct funds			

Notice that there isn't much difference in the return for the top six funds. However, the twelfth fund is a full percentage point lower at 6.47 per cent. Clearly, we need to look for funds in the top two quartiles and look at some other factors as well. Next, we look at the five-year return data in Table 10.11.

Table 10.11

Five-year ranks and performance			
	Name	Rank	Return (%)
1	Fund 4	1/12	6.37
2	Fund 6	2/12	6.29
3	Fund 7	3/12	6.25
4	Fund 1	4/12	6.20
5	Fund 8	5/12	6.19
6	Fund 9	6/12	6.15
All direct funds			

Over a five-year period, the difference in return in the top quartile is beginning to show. Funds 1, 4 and 6 are still in the top two quartiles, though Fund 1 has dropped to the fourth place now. We next look at three-year data in Table 10.12.

Table 10.12

Three-year ranks and performance			
	Name	Rank	Return (%)
1	Fund 10	1/16	5.24
2	Fund 4	2/16	5.22
3	Fund 6	3/16	5.19
4	Fund 11	4/16	5.07
5	Fund 7	5/16	5.02
6	Fund 9	6/16	5.00
7	Fund 8	7/16	4.99
8	Fund 1	8/16	4.98
All direct funds			

The three-year data has many schemes that are showing top two quartile returns that continue. Funds 1, 4 and 6 are still there, but see that Fund 1 is getting lower and lower on performance, it barely makes it to the second quartile. Table 10.13 gives the one-year return data and there are now twenty schemes in this category.

Table 10.13

One-year ranks and performance			
	Name	Rank	Return (%)
1	Fund 7	1/20	5.18
2	Fund 10	2/20	5.14
3	Fund 12	3/20	5.07
4	Fund 8	4/20	5.06
5	Fund 4	5/20	5.04
6	Fund 13	6/20	5.02
7	Fund 11	7/20	5.01
8	Fund 6	8/20	5.00
9	Fund 9	9/20	4.93
10	Fund 1	10/20	4.92
All direct funds			

We are beginning to see some names show up often, Funds 1, 4 and 6 are holding their heads above water in terms of continuing with top-two quartile returns over time. Table 10.14 gives the six-month performance ranks.

Table 10.14

Six-month ranks and performance			
	Name	Rank	Return (%)
1	Fund 10	1/20	3.08
2	Fund 7	2/20	3.06
3	Fund 4	3/20	3.04
4	Fund 6	4/20	3.01
5	Fund 8	5/20	3.01
6	Fund 9	6/20	2.99
7	Fund 11	7/20	2.99
8	Fund 12	8/20	2.99
9	Fund 1	9/20	2.98
10	Fund 13	10/20	2.96
All direct funds			

All the schemes in the top two quartiles have been there before in the past. There is a very small difference in returns, but the persistency of performance of funds is quite clear. So, we look at how many funds have been in the top two quartiles over all the time periods in Table 10.15.

Table 10.15

How to map consistency of performance	
Fund 1	Makes the cut across all time periods
Fund 4	Makes the cut across all time periods
Fund 6	Makes the cut across all time periods
Fund 7	Makes the cut in three out of five time periods
Fund 9	Makes the cut in three out of five time periods

How to map consistency of performance	
Fund 10	Makes the cut in three out of five time periods
Fund 11	Makes the cut in three out of five time periods

Funds 1, 4 and 6 make it to the top quartile over all the time periods we looked at. But we will keep all seven funds just to see if there is some other factor that might do better on the risk and cost metric. The difference in returns is a few basis points and we need to put these through the filter of risk-grade persistency and expense-ratio efficiency.

The Risk-o-Meter is a useful pointer to the risk on the metrics of liquidity, interest rate and credit risk. Go back and read page 154 in Chapter 7 for details on how to use the Risk-o-Meter. Table 10.16 gives the Risk-o-Meter readings against each shortlisted scheme at the time of this exercise.

Table 10.16

Risk-o-Meter	
Fund 1	Moderate
Fund 4	Moderate
Fund 6	Moderate
Fund 7	Moderate
Fund 9	Moderate
Fund 10	Moderate
Fund 11	Moderate

All funds are reporting a moderate risk metric on the Risk-o-Meter. We need to monitor this risk level over time and therefore, we turn to a SEBI rule that says that the mutual fund houses need to disclose the changes in the Risk-o-Meter reading over the financial year. While this is of little use in equity funds since they are all marked high risk, this is very useful in the debt fund category that can see the credit quality and duration of the portfolio change drastically over time. We turn to AMFI that has links to all the fund houses that should display the change in the risk handle.[5]

The change in the Risk-o-Meter is documented in Table 10.17. We find that some fund houses have not updated this data or are not making it easy to find the changes in the Risk-o-Meter. This is a really important metric in debt funds and poor disclosure of data is reason enough to reject a shortlisted scheme.

Table 10.17

Change in Risk-o-Meter FY22	
Fund 1	0
Fund 4	0
Fund 6	0
Fund 7	2 (FY21 data)
Fund 9	2
Fund 10	0 (FY21 data)
Fund 11	1

The fact that the industry does not listen to the regulator is manifest when you begin digging a bit into the innards of data. While funds 1, 4, 6, 9 and 11 reported the Risk-o-Meter for FY22, two funds were displaying previous year data. Not displaying this data is a negative against the fund when you are choosing. The data is also showing that Funds, 1, 4 and 6 saw no change in the risk marking over FY22—that is a plus.

Now we need to look at the expense ratios. Cost matters in debt funds because returns are thin and an expensive fund can eat into your returns. The chosen schemes are displaying similar cost numbers in Table 10.18.

Table 10.18

Expense ratio	
Fund 10	0.17
Fund 4	0.21
Fund 6	0.21
Fund 7	0.21
Fund 9	0.21
Fund 11	0.21
Fund 1	0.23

While cost does matter, the cheapest may not be the best. Fund 1 is the most expensive and Fund 10 the cheapest in the shortlisted funds. The range for all funds of cost is between 0.26 per cent and 0.13 per cent—so most of the chosen funds are towards the higher end of the cost metric. Since we like the performance consistency and the risk ratings, we prefer to pay higher expense ratios than the cheapest funds in the market.

Choosing a scheme

Money market funds are not bought for their high returns. Nor for being the least expensive. The returns, cost and risk mostly look similar on all seven funds. The expense ratios are similar too.

I will choose from Funds 1, 4 and 6 as they make the performance grade over time, have similar expense ratios and have seen no change in the Risk-o-Meter over FY22. Fund 4 is showing top quartile performance with the same risk as the other two, with an expense ratio that is marginally lower than Fund 1. Given that the funds are so similar in their risk and cost profiles, it makes sense to now go for the fund with the highest return consistency in this group of shortlisted three.

See that I am trying to give you a path to scheme selection. I am not giving you a list of funds to buy, I am giving you a process, a recipe that you can use and modify according to your needs. This data would have changed for the funds I shortlisted and the names might look very different two years later. So, do not try and guess the scheme names, but use that time to understand the process and then do the exercise yourself.

Choosing schemes is not an easy task. But if you do this exercise over and over again to select the six to ten schemes an average portfolio needs, you will get well versed in the process. Once you have your set of schemes, then it is an annual audit to see if there is a major change in the trajectory of the scheme or the fund house. One bad year does not mean you abandon the scheme.

That was hard work. But what we got is a system that does not rely on a huge amount of data processing that can work for a first-time mutual fund investor. There are several ways to use worksheets and data sets to run these numbers, but few people have the ability to work complicated Excel sheets. You will never have the top-performing scheme across all time periods, but you will have a consistent performer over ten-to-twenty years with reasonable risk and cost metrics.

The easier category of funds to choose out of is index funds. These are great products for people who do not want to spend time and effort to select active funds. But selecting an index fund is getting more and more difficult. Let's get a method in the next chapter.

It is not easy to choose schemes and it is important to have a process you can manage on your own. There is a middle ground to crunching vast amounts of data on an ongoing basis and buying every tip you get. Having a system in place to choose funds also gives you a better understanding of the way your distributor or planner is coming to their lists of schemes.

You are doing okay if you understand that

1. return consistency is very important in a scheme;
2. the top-performing scheme in one year can be the worst the next year;
3. a scheme that stays consistently in the top quartile is a good candidate;
4. it must do well on metrics of risk in comparison to others in the shortlist;
5. it must do well on cost as compared to others selected; and
6. the Risk-o-Meter is very important for debt schemes.

11

INDEX INVESTING

There are no easy roads. There are roads that are easier than others.

Index funds are a great option if you don't want to do all the work laid out in Chapter 10 and do not want fund manager risk. You want a fill it–shut it–forget it approach to your money decisions. There are plenty of studies that show that passive investors on the whole do better than active fund investors. You could use both active and passive funds as parts of your overall equity portfolio. But passive fund investing too needs some work, and as you read the next part, you are going to say: this was supposed to be the easy road to fund selection and here we are dealing with choice overload and data all over again. I will give you simple ways to cut the clutter and reduce your decision steps to just a few. But belt up, it still needs attention and work.

Refresh your understanding of an index and passive investing from *Let's Talk Money* Chapters 8 and 9.

We set out to invest in an index fund, but run into the first roadblock—which index should we mimic? There are seventy-one indices on the NSE to choose from.[1] Let's reduce the choice set here. The simplest passive investing strategy is to simply follow one of the two oldest broad-market indices on the Indian stock market. Broad market means that the index stocks account for some of the largest and best-known companies on the stock market. The S&P BSE Sensex has thirty stocks and the Nifty 50 has fifty stocks that make up the index. With over twenty-five years of data available, it is easy to back-test the returns on these two indices. The long history and their use as bellwether indices also means that there are more schemes around these indices than other newer ones, giving investors a larger choice set than, say, a newer bespoke index constructed for a much narrower market segment. For example, the Nifty alpha low-volatility 30 index has just two schemes that track it.

Also notice that fund manager style is embedded into some bespoke indices and can be very risky for you. Pure passive investing needs to step away from such indices and schemes—you are better off investing in a managed fund rather than step into what you think is a safe passive fund only to find out that it is following a certain investment style or strategy. Getting turbulence in what you thought was a safe ride is worse than facing it if you are already belted up for it.

Follow these steps to choose your index fund.

Step one. Choose only from index funds and not ETFs. The ETFs are listed like stocks and when you go to buy or sell, there has to be somebody on the other side making the opposite trade. While there are market makers whose job is to provide liquidity, there can be instances that you go to sell and there aren't enough buyers. Index funds are different—the units are sold and bought by the mutual fund itself. The fund house has to buy back whatever you are selling at the applicable NAV. Unless there is a major market calamity, such as the crash of March 2020 when redemptions of some debt funds was frozen, the Indian mutual fund market has not seen a situation where the investor was not able to sell all the units of a scheme when she wanted to. Mutual funds keep a buffer of cash to meet investors' redemption demands. So, we stay only with index funds and remove ETFs from the long list of passive funds out there.

Step two. Reduce the choice of index funds to only those that track the bellwether indices. These are Nifty 50 and the S&P BSE Sensex and both indices show very similar return history. You can look at the long list of these funds on the AMFI site.[2] You can also use Value Research and Money Control for a list of passive funds. There will be other data sets out there—use the one that you trust with data today and the confidence that the data source will be alive in the future.

Shortlist all schemes that have S&P BSE Sensex total return index and Nifty 50 total return index as the benchmarks. Remove the ETFs from this list and keep only the index funds. There is a 'download Excel' option on the page that you can use to create your own sheet. Out of 185 passive funds, we are left with just twenty-three index funds, the rest are ETFs. Of these, just five are on the S&P BSE Sensex and the rest on Nifty 50. You can see the shortlisted names in Table 11.1. I am not taking the names of the schemes even though there is very little personal discretion in finally picking the scheme. There isn't much one can do to nudge investor choice when we are dealing with index funds, but I will still not mention names here. Again, remember that the list will increase as newer funds begin to offer broad market index funds. The data is from Value Research.

Table 11.1

Index funds on the Sensex and Nifty 50			
	Scheme name	Benchmark	AUM (Rs crore)
1	Fund 1 Nifty 50 index fund	Nifty 50 total return index	510.62
2	Fund 2 Nifty 50 index fund	Nifty 50 total return index	195.18
3	Fund 3 Nifty 50 index fund	Nifty 50 total return index	259.04

Index funds on the Sensex and Nifty 50			
	Scheme name	Benchmark	AUM (Rs crore)
4	Fund 4 Nifty 50 index fund	Nifty 50 total return index	11.21
5	Fund 5 Nifty 50 index fund	Nifty 50 total return index	497.13
6	Fund 6 Nifty 50 index fund	Nifty 50 total return index	7,429.25
7	Fund 7 Nifty 50 index fund	Nifty 50 total return index	137.05
8	Fund 8 Nifty 50 index fund	Nifty 50 total return index	3,935.36
9	Fund 9 Nifty 50 index fund	Nifty 50 total return index	199.56
10	Fund 10 Nifty 50 index fund	Nifty 50 total return index	585.44
11	Fund 11 Nifty 50 index fund	Nifty 50 total return index	253.76
12	Fund 12 Nifty 50 index fund	Nifty 50 total return index	53.15
13	Fund 13 Nifty 50 index fund	Nifty 50 total return index	228.78
14	Fund 14 Nifty 50 index fund	Nifty 50 total return index	633.61
15	Fund 15 Nifty 50 index fund	Nifty 50 total return index	631.74
16	Fund 16 Nifty 50 index fund	Nifty 50 total return index	3,221.01

Index funds on the Sensex and Nifty 50			
	Scheme name	Benchmark	AUM (Rs crore)
17	Fund 17 Nifty 50 index fund	Nifty 50 total return index	359.44
18	Fund 18 Nifty 50 index fund	Nifty 50 total return index	9,407.45
19	Fund 19 S&P BSE Sensex fund	S&P BSE Sensex total return index	4,150.77
20	Fund 20 Nifty 50 index fund	S&P BSE Sensex total return index	643.47
21	Fund 21 Nifty 50 index fund	S&P BSE Sensex total return index	69.45
22	Fund 22 Nifty 50 index fund	S&P BSE Sensex total return index	363.53
23	Fund 23 Nifty 50 index fund	S&P BSE Sensex total return index	171.96

Step three. Use the filter of assets under management to remove schemes that are small. We are looking for a scheme with performance history and a minimum size of at least Rs 500 crore. Smaller funds, if not new, might suffer from the problem of lack of attention of the fund house. Tiny, old passive funds must be avoided, these are obviously neglected by the fund house. Using this filter, we have just ten schemes left to choose from as in Table 11.2. Once the number or schemes in the top ten grow, use a tighter filter of Rs 1,000 crore as the investments increase in passive funds, and so on.

Table 11.2

Index funds on Sensex and Nifty 50 ranked by AUM			
	Scheme name	Benchmark	AUM (Rs crore)
1	Fund 18	Nifty 50 total return index	9,407.45
2	Fund 6	Nifty 50 total return index	7,429.25
3	Fund 19	S&P BSE Sensex total return index	4,150.77
4	Fund 8	Nifty 50 total return index	3,935.36
5	Fund 16	Nifty 50 total return index	3,221.01
6	Fund 20	S&P BSE Sensex total return index	643.47
7	Fund 14	Nifty 50 total return index	633.61
8	Fund 15	Nifty 50 total return index	631.74
9	Fund 10	Nifty 50 total return index	585.44
10	Fund 1	Nifty 50 total return index	510.62

Step four. We now look at the expense ratios to find lower cost schemes within the group. The cheapest may not be the best because we need to see how well the scheme does in hugging the index. We see this in Table 11.3. Notice that expense ratios are very different across Number 1 and Number 10. We need to check on how well the passive fund is hugging the index next.

Table 11.3

Index funds ranked by expense ratio			
	Scheme name	Expense ratio (%)	AUM (Rs crore)
1	Fund 14	0.06	633.61
2	Fund 10	0.10	585.44
3	Fund 8	0.17	3,935.36
4	Fund 16	0.18	3,221.01
5	Fund 18	0.20	9,407.45
6	Fund 6	0.20	7,429.25
7	Fund 19	0.20	4,150.77
8	Fund 15	0.20	631.74
9	Fund 20	0.29	643.47
10	Fund 1	0.32	510.62

Step five. Check if the passive fund is actually doing its job. You use a measure called tracking error to find if you are getting index returns or not. You can look for tracking error data on the AMFI site on an ongoing basis.[3]

The definition of tracking error is technical, but here goes: it is the annualized standard deviation of the difference in returns between the index fund and its target index. What it means is that tracking error measures how far the scheme performance is from the index it tracks. Ideally there should be no difference—plus or minus—because the mandate from the investor is to replicate index returns. The lower this error metric, the closer is the scheme performance to the index.

One of the reasons for a larger tracking error is a higher expense ratio. If the scheme expense ratio is high, then the returns will show a larger deviation from index returns. Another reason is that the fund has to maintain a cash balance to service redemptions and this reduces the money that is deployed in index stocks causing a divergence of return from the index. In Table 11.4, the data on AUM, expense ratio and tracking error is together in one place.

We are now down to six schemes as I am letting go of schemes with a tracking error greater than 0.10 per cent.

Table 11.4

Index funds ranked by tracking error				
	Scheme name	Expense ratio (%)	AUM (Rs crore)	Tracking error (%)
1	Fund 16	0.18	3,221.01	0.03
2	Fund 18	0.20	9,407.45	0.03
3	Fund 6	0.20	7,429.25	0.04
4	Fund 19	0.20	4,150.77	0.04
5	Fund 14	0.06	633.61	0.04
6	Fund 8	0.17	3,935.36	0.07

A scheme with a large AUM, at least five years data availability of various metrics, low tracking error and low expense ratio is just fine. It need not be the lowest since this metric will change with time. This is not a list of recommended schemes in any way. The data on AUM, expense ratios and tracking errors will change over time. This is a way to show a process to you so that you can do this yourself. The data links allow you to download the names, metrics and shortlist the scheme that will stay with you for almost the rest of your investing life.

Remember that it is really important to pick a scheme with a good track record of keeping its expense ratio low and maintaining a low tracking error over time because there is a cost to moving from one scheme to another in terms of a capital gains tax. Till the time that the tax department fixes this problem of taxing the profits as you reallocate within the same asset class, the choice of the scheme becomes even more important.

We've now got a method to shortlist categories and within them, schemes. Now we will build some model portfolios in the next chapter.

Index funds are a great choice for a new investor to taste equity funds. They also work for the investor who does not want to track active funds and is okay to have just the market average return. Broad market index funds are a good way to secure the safer part of your equity portfolio.

You are doing okay if you understand that

1. staying with Sensex or Nifty 50 index funds is a great long-term equity strategy;
2. you will just get an average market return, nothing above that;
3. staying away from indices you do not understand is a good idea;
4. index funds must be low on expense ratio
5. they must be low on tracking error; and
6. debt index funds are a new entity and will take time to have more options.

12

PORTFOLIOS

The spiritual mantra 'the only thing you can control is yourself' translates beautifully into investing—the only thing you control is your asset allocation.

I still get asked this question and I still don't know how to answer it: tell me five funds to invest in. I usually just suggest that they read *Let's Talk Money*. How do I tell them that it is not certain that the five funds I name today will do equally well a decade later? How do I tell them that portfolio creation needs far more care than a tip from somebody you meet at a party?

How do I tell them that they are destroying their financial future by asking for and implementing some casual recommendation? I'm sure I end up seeming arrogant or just not helpful when I refuse to answer. But my fiduciary duty—the duty of care—towards a financially naive person is such that I would risk this opinion rather than lead them up some path that will certainly not end well. One route I do allow for is to recommend that they invest in passive or index funds on a broad market index like the S&P BSE Sensex or Nifty 50. But let's get to that point in just a bit.

This is the chapter that puts to use all that we have done till now. We are at the stage of creating portfolios that contain mainly mutual funds. Mainly? Yes, let's see what that means further into the chapter.

Portfolios are very personal and individual collections of assets that are designed to make available money to you at a future date from today. A portfolio of a seventy-five-year old single man with no children, and on a lifetime pension, will be very different than one for a similar aged person, with a dependent wife. In one case, there will be a desire to create a corpus for bequeathing to his favourite niece and in the other a very heavy allocation to current income.

Solving the asset-allocation problem

The first decision you have to take when you think of building your portfolio is to solve for the allocation of money between debt and equity. I cannot stress how key this decision is for your entire financial life. The debt part of the portfolio is your life jacket whether in shallow waters or deep. This is always on. The debt part of the portfolio caters for short-term liquidity and long-term stability of the portfolio against the volatility of equity.

The next question is: in what proportion do I hold these various asset classes? There are many rules of thumb about how much equity is enough in your portfolio. In *Let's Talk Money*, I have used the '100 minus your age' idea to know your equity allocation according to age. At age eighty, you are still 20 per cent in equity. At age forty, you should be 60 per cent in equity.

While this rule of thumb is useful as a mental marker, there is one more way to think through this question. Use the distance from today that the goal sits at to decide your allocation. For immediate needs, you need cash in the bank. For money needs within three years, 100 per cent in debt instruments. For needs between three to seven years, a sliding scale between debt and equity. Closer to three years is more debt, closer to seven years is more equity. Stay within the approximate range of 10 per cent to 50 per cent equity across the time period. Use a sliding scale of equity for goals further than seven years. Starting with 50 per cent and going all the way to 100 per cent equity. For money needs more than ten years away, go all the way into equity.

There will always be a better strategy, a better fund, a better return out there. There will always be people telling you that you are not doing enough. How you missed out on some great return opportunity. Instead of letting it destabilize you, just ask one small question: what is your portfolio return? Across debt and equity and across all the products—what is that one number in CAGR? This is a simple but powerful way to get back to a balance when being told tall stories of return opportunities you might have missed.

I was meeting a regional head of a big wealth-management firm after many years. As we caught up, she began telling me of all the super good fund managers they find. How they find the next Prashant Jain (the star ex-HDFC fund manager) before he gets known. On and on about the higher alpha and the higher return. Finally, I asked her, 'so what is it that at a portfolio level you return over the Sensex?' Oh, two or three percentage points, she tossed nonchalantly. I'm sure, by now I don't need to tell you that all this song and dance and higher fees does not justify this outperformance.

Displaying your wins on some money bets in a social situation is a very alpha male conversation style. Stay away from such talk. Choose carefully and then don't let the money motormouths shake you off your plan. They are everywhere on all the social media channels and sites telling you how only they have the strategy for lifetime high returns.

Be careful of product placement of raw untested advice on these sources.

Portfolios

In each of the following portfolios, you have to do your own asset allocation depending on your needs for money spread over time. I stay with a basic portfolio division between equity and debt to create these here. Within the debt part, there is an allocation to the long-term assets such as PF and PPF and shorter term ones such as FDs and debt funds.

Within equity, there is an allocation between index funds, across market caps and foreign funds.

The five portfolios here can be the starting point for your own journey as you use this framework to make your own unique portfolio to solve your own unique problems. The portfolios go from very low risk at level one to very high risk at level five.

Level one: equity index funds + PF + PPF + FDs

This is an entry-level portfolio allocation. It aims to help an investor new to mutual funds begin onboarding using a lower risk route. Think of this as the shallow end of the pool and you have a life jacket just in case you panic and go under. There have been cases of people drowning even in a bathtub, let alone the shallow end of a swimming pool—up to a quarter of drownings happen in the shallow end of the pool. Therefore, I am putting a life jacket of secure products as part of the portfolio.

Money needs in five years or less are kept in fixed deposits. Debt funds take some work before you can use them, so I will keep them for a higher risk profile. Retirement money is in your PF account and in the PPF in which you are allowed to invest up to Rs 1.5 lakh a year. Both contributions get you the Section 80C tax deduction. Both investments are tax free when you get the money back—there is no tax on interest during the period and no tax on your gains on exit. These two remain a gift of the Indian government to middle-class India. Use them.

For those who do not have the benefit of PF from their work—you are a gig worker or have taken the consultant route while being employed full time—you need to pretend that 12 per cent of your average monthly income is being invested for your retirement. The PF contribution of people in an organized sector job is 12 per cent of basic that is matched by 12 per cent employer contribution. That makes it 24 per cent of basic salary. Basic salary is usually 40–50 per cent of the CTC on an average. So, the gig worker needs to salt away 12 per cent of her average monthly income flows towards retirement.

There is no easy way to replace the PF part of the long-term debt allocation by an individual. The National Pension System is a great option but on retirement, 40 per cent of the corpus is forced to buy an annuity from an insurance company. The annuity market in India is not that great and that means you give up control over 40 per cent of your retirement money. This could change in the years ahead, but as in April 2023, I will still advise you to use an index fund on the Nifty 50 or Sensex to target your retirement corpus if it is more than ten years away.

For an investor who has never tasted mutual funds, an index fund is a great way to begin on the equity side. I cannot repeat this enough: equity investing through mutual funds is much easier than debt fund investing. Choose your index fund carefully (read Chapter 11 again) and then just stay with it for your entire long-term investing journey. This is the easiest, safest, cheapest route to long-term wealth creation.

Level two: equity index funds + PF + PPF + FDs + debt funds

We begin to introduce a bit more risk into the portfolio by swapping FDs for debt funds for some purposes. The equity part stays the same as level one, with only one index fund for long-term accumulation.

For money needs that are within six months away, use the sweep facility into an FD if your bank gives it, else just let it sit in a savings deposit. The certainty of the money being there when you need it is greater than the desire for a higher return. It is a mindset change and you must make it to prevent sleepless nights that will happen when you target high returns in the very short term.

Your emergency funds continue to be in a fixed deposit of a large public or private sector bank. Stay away from corporate deposits and cooperative bank deposits even though they might give you a higher interest. Higher return always, always, always comes with higher risk. An emergency fund is sometimes food and basic bills money. You do not mess with that on safety for a higher return.

Now, take a leap away from FDs and allocate into debt funds for our short- and medium-term needs. Use money market funds for needs up to two years away and banking and PSU bond funds for money needs within two-to-seven years. Go back to Chapter 10 to remind yourself of the process to shortlist the scheme that makes it to your portfolio. Always compare with the return being offered by your bank on the FDs when looking at time periods between one to five years.

There are times when bank FDs do better and it is good to lock into higher rates if you can.

Level three: equity index funds + active funds + PF + PPF + FDs + debt funds

You are now going to wade into the middle of the pool where your toes might just get off the ground, but you are still hugging the edges of the pool so as to be within arm's length from the safety of the side wall.

Equity allocation

This is the portfolio that begins to introduce some managed funds into your money box. I will start with a 50 per cent index, 25 per cent aggressive hybrid and 25 per cent large- and mid-cap allocation. If you were investing Rs 100 in equity, then half the money is still going to an index fund on the Sensex or Nifty 50. A quarter of your equity allocation goes to an aggressive hybrid fund that invests between 65 per cent and 80 per cent in equity and the rest in debt. The debt part gives stability and lowers the risk. Go back to Chapter 10 to remind yourself of the process to shortlist the scheme that makes it to your portfolio. A quarter of your equity allocation goes to one large- and mid-cap scheme that invests a minimum of 35 per cent each in large- and mid-cap stocks. Most of these funds have 35 per cent in mid-cap stocks and the rest in large-cap stocks to reduce the risk. This is a higher risk category than large-cap, but we are already doing half the money in an index fund, so as a proportion of your entire portfolio, mid-cap stocks are under 10 per cent of your entire equity allocation. You have to be careful to select schemes that outperform the benchmark by following the process diligently.

Debt allocation

You can continue to keep your emergency funds in a fixed deposit. Your PF and PPF flows keep going. You continue to use money market and banking and PSU bond funds for money needs that are further than six months away. You can now begin to use liquid funds for keeping money liquid for use within six months. Once you connect your bank to the platform, the redemption from a liquid fund, if done before 3 p.m. of a market-open day, takes just a day. Notice that I have left one of the safest products in the debt fund space for the end. Why? Because unless you have fully understood the use of debt funds, I cannot put your very near-term money at risk at all.

Level four: equity index + active multi-cap funds + PF + PPF + debt funds

You are now well on your way to the deep end of the pool. You've learnt to swim fairly well but you are not taking chances and will keep your long-term safe debt jacket on even here. You will play safe and not try to walk on the bottom of the pool—leave that for the hedge fund managers.

Equity allocation

You have a choice of several approaches here. One, stay with 50 per cent index, 25 per cent mid-cap and 25 per cent small-cap funds. The index fund gives your portfolio long-term stable returns, the mid- and small-cap funds add the return kicker. Both mid- and small-cap are far more volatile and can go through longish periods of poor performance, but when the bounce-back happens, and you have the right scheme, the portfolio returns look very good.

Two, allocate 40 per cent to index funds and 60 per cent to two multi-cap funds. Multi-cap funds must invest a minimum of 25 per cent each in large-, mid- and small-cap stocks. This is an easier journey than the first one since your choice set is now down to just two active funds. We use two to diversify across fund houses.

Three, 25 per cent each in index, large- and mid-cap, mid-cap and small-cap schemes. I personally prefer the first approach because it allows me to choose the consistent mid- and small-cap schemes for my own portfolio. But you do you!

Debt allocation

The debt allocation does not change from the earlier level. You have to keep looking out for a change in the Risk-o-Meter reading when you take the path of active debt funds. I like liquid funds for my short-term money needs, to park some funds before I deploy and to just hold money that I do not need immediately. The money is moved away from sitting in your savings deposit asking to be spent or lent away. The additional roadblock of having to redeem to use the money is like a cool-off period before spending.

Level five: equity index + active multi-cap + foreign funds + PF + PPF + debt funds

This level is for a sophisticated investor whose portfolio is large enough to need diversification across geographies. Geographical diversification helps reduce the own-country bias that most home-only portfolios suffer from. Especially in areas like technology, an exposure to the US tech sector (which includes all the new AI, robotics, neuroscience and their convergence-related enterprises) is good for the portfolio. But there are problems of adding this diversification of access and taxation. While there are a few fund houses that directly manage an offshore fund, most take the fund of funds routes. The Indian mutual fund will own one or more schemes of an offshore fund.

There are two problems with this. One, you pay the expense ratio of the scheme you buy and that of the funds it owns. So, it is very important when choosing schemes to understand the overall expense ratio. Some fund houses give an expense ratio that includes the cost of the overseas scheme and some do not.

Two, the taxation rules strangely count even equity fund of funds as a debt product and are taxed accordingly. There is reform imminent in this area of taxation so do keep checking the AMFI site for the latest tax provisions.[1]

Foreign funds are off the Risk-o-Meter in terms of their risk marking since they are marked at risk level 7 in a mapping that ends at risk level 6. So be careful and only step out once you have a mutual fund holding of at least 1 crore before you take this risk.

Begin by an allocation of 10 per cent to foreign funds of your total equity portfolio.

How many schemes should a portfolio have?

Each portfolio level will differ on the schemes. Starting with a basic level of just one scheme as in an equity index fund, to no more than six to ten schemes in a level five portfolio. Do not buy too many similar schemes in the same category—you end up buying the index at a much higher cost. I have seen this typical investor behaviour—they carefully dip their toes with one or two schemes and if the market is on a bull run, they soon think that they are experts. Two years later, their portfolio has more than twenty-five schemes. They buy everything anybody recommends. Each scheme must justify its place in your money box. There is limited space—let the funds compete to be a part of your portfolio. Do not gorge on everything being sold; instead, use chopsticks to carefully pick the one that works for you and your needs.

Portfolio construction

The first time you make your portfolio, allocate plenty of time for it. Take up to three months to do it. Anything longer and it gets to be at the end of the to-do list. From start to finish, take time out on your weekends to do this. First, identify your needs and split them into short, medium and long term. Then plan your asset allocation between debt and equity.

Next, choose one of the portfolios described above or one that you have found and liked. Now begin to fill the portfolio with schemes. Follow the process in Chapters 10 and 11 for choosing the scheme. Go through the process of checking performance, consistency, risk and cost. Plan to stay with the scheme for the very long term and change it only if there is a consistent underperformance or a change in your life stage and needs.

Basic hygiene for a good portfolio

There can be hundreds of approaches across tens of portfolios. There will never be the perfect portfolio and you should not wait for one. Like Sima Aunty of Indian Matchmaking says: there is never 100 per cent of what you want, 70 per cent milega to chalega. Not seen that Netflix series yet? Go for it—the most feet-on-the-ground approach to a marriage I have seen on screen. Think of your portfolio and schemes in the same way—you will never get a consistent scheme that stays at number one. Be happy with a set of funds that stay in the top quartile most of the time, slipping to the second quartile now and then.

When should you book profit?

Another way to look at this question is a more stable one—when should you rebalance your portfolio? Rebalance when one of the two things happen. One, there is change in your age, stage or needs. As you move towards a time period where your current spending needs are being partly or fully met from the income arising out of your assets, you will need to change your asset allocation to be heavier in debt than equity. When you have a long runway ahead of you of income through current work or a job, you can assign a higher allocation to equity, but that changes as you age. Be alert to changes in your personal situation and modify your portfolio accordingly. A way to do this, without having to book profits, is to funnel incremental investments into the asset class that needs to be enhanced. That way you do not have to pay capital gains tax just to rebalance.

Two, the asset allocation you had chosen has changed due to a bull or a bear phase in the market. Suppose you begin with an asset allocation that you are comfortable at 70:30. That is 70 per cent equity and 30 per cent debt. This might not even be the allocation of those in their thirties; it might even be that of somebody in their sixties who has enough capital and the 30 per cent debt more than looks after their needs for the next decade at the least. Over time, the equity market run-up takes their equity allocation all the way up to 80 per cent or higher. This is the time to sell equity (book profits) and buy debt to return to the chosen 70:30.

During 2021, the markets had run up after the 2020 crash and many allocations were equity heavy. I remember selling equity funds all through the summer to winter of 2021 to return to my chosen allocation. It is not easy to sell when markets are high, but each time I have personally followed the rebalance rule, I have thanked my younger self which took that decision!

If the allocation is mildly off, then instead of booking profits and having to pay capital gains tax, you can simply increase the debt allocation of fresh investments. But rebalance you must.

Good time to invest in ...

Gold, mid-cap funds, small-cap funds, liquid funds? The question haunts me, very similar to the five funds one. I have no way to answer this, except point to data that shows every year has a different category winner. For example, in 2014, the small-cap stocks outperformed all other categories and asset classes. But by 2016, they were the worst performing category.

The year 2017 saw them being back at the top and then two years of worst category. International funds were at the top in 2013 and 2019 and at the bottom in 2022. Every year throws up a new winner and last year's winner can be this year's loser. There is no good time to be in this or that. You have to be in all the categories that you have chosen all the time. Please just forget about moving in and out of categories and funds. You will never make money by bouncing around buying last year's winners.

What a good portfolio construction does is to free you from having to decide every few months on what to do with fresh money. Suppose you have a 50:25:25 portfolio between an index fund, a mid- and a small-cap fund. Now you suddenly get Rs 6 lakh as an annual bonus. What to do with it? Assuming you want to invest all of it and not a bit of retail therapy, then the 6 lakh gets divided in the same ratio. Rs 3 lakh goes into the index fund, Rs 1.5 lakh each in the mid- and the small-cap. You don't buy new schemes, you just add to what you have already chosen.

Your asset allocation is your one true anchor in your investing life. You need to fix this when markets are down to get a real understanding of your true risk appetite. A portfolio approach is the right way to think about investing as it frees you from bragging about your winners and stressing about your losers.

You are doing okay if you understand that

1. there is no best return, and what wins today might lose tomorrow;
2. you need to make an overall asset allocation;
3. you need to pick categories first;
4. you then have to pick funds;
5. you must stay with the portfolio; and
6. you rebalance when asset allocation changes or when life situation changes.

13

HOW TO BUY

Without a system in place, the repetitive actions that adulting requires will make the journey all about processes and tasks rather than experiences.

I have a set procedure for my travel. I start to gather all the things I need to take with me in a particular cupboard or place in the house. This includes documents, gifts, specific items of clothing needed for the trip, papers for the meeting, if any, and so on. The suitcases are packed on the day of travel and, mostly, I don't miss anything important. We all have protocols we follow for the repetitive tasks that we perform. I use a mix of brain triggers and planning to get things right. You need to think of the rest of your investing life in a similar manner so that you don't need to spend the same time each instance you need to invest or redeem.

Follow the simple rules I put out and you will not need more than one minute to execute the investments, switches or redemptions. Planning can take a lot of time, but execution needs to be swift, least cost and non-stressful. When I am rebalancing, I actually have the names of funds ready to both exit and enter, so that execution gets done. We get busy with the dramas that life throws at us and unless the task is defined, simple and a habit, it will remain not done.

The next few pages will prepare you to begin your investing journey into mutual funds in a planned, systematic way. You are getting set for a lifetime of investing, redeeming and maintaining, so set it up with good foundations.

Documents

You need some form of an identity document before you are allowed to board an aircraft. The name and face are matched with the Aadhaar card, driving license or passport you offer at the gate. Fly overseas and you need a visa—a stamp from the country you are visiting. They want to know who you are, where you live and a whole bunch of other stuff like income, profession, whether you have funds for your stay and purpose of visit. The overseas country is trying to ascertain that you will not either be a part of a terrorist network or dissolve into their country as an illegal immigrant while being on a tourist visa. While this does not prevent either of the two, it does increase the cost of time and money for everybody else. But you end up bearing that cost and irritation, and doing the paperwork because you want to travel for personal or business reasons.

Think of the onboarding process of a mutual fund as very similar to that of getting a visa to travel. That visa is called a know-your-customer (KYC) process. For a KYC, you need your PAN details and Aadhar. Many other documents such as driving license and passport are also allowed, but if you have your Aadhaar and are not growing and trading in weed or some other illegal stuff, use it. Once your general KYC is complete, you don't need to get it done for every new fund house you buy a scheme from. The PAN–Aadhaar combination is a useful one in most of your other paperwork as well. I am assuming that if you are reading this book, you have a bank account. Not just one, but three—Income Account, where all your money inflows drop, Spend-It account, where you move the money you will spend in the month, and Invest-It account, which holds your savings that wait to get invested away from the temptation of being spent and lent.

Get your Invest-It account ready to make your first transaction through the bank. You can get your bank to do the KYC, or do it directly yourself. Google it as newer ways to get this done keep emerging. I dislike the bank option for investing because they put you in a regular plan without any of the services, either those that a platform provides or the portfolio-creation help that some large distributors give. Most bank customers' mutual fund portfolios have too many schemes that do not add up to a coherent portfolio. So, get your KYC done and then use a DIY platform that gives you a direct plan to transact.

Alternatively, if you are investing through a distributor, financial advisor or platform, use them to facilitate your KYC process. Most of them do it for free in the anticipation of getting a payback from the trail commission if you are in a regular plan, through transaction fees or simply by increasing their valuation by showing a large community of investors to the venture capitalists. You will pay one way or the other, though at the moment most people are preferring that their data (personal details) is harvested than paying for any of these services. These are the choices we make.

The rules around KYC keep changing over the years and you are better off going to the AMFI site to look at the update rather than read old information in a book. Essentially, you need four things to start your investing journey into mutual funds—bank account, PAN, Aadhaar and KYC. And, of course, savings.

Routes

The innovation (and regulation) in the mutual fund industry and its allied services is fast and developments happen frequently. I am going to keep it very simple and stay with basic approaches to the routes you can take rather than get specific on what is out there. Your first choice is to decide whether to go with a distributor or a platform with a regular plan or do it yourself and go direct? Or will you take a third option where you use the services of a fee-only financial planner who takes an annual fee and buys the lower cost direct plans for you?

The DIY route

My grandmother used to quote a Hindi phrase that goes like this: doodh aur poot ka kaam kabhi samapt nahin hota—the work around milk and child is never over. Investing is similar. The work is never over. It is not enough to just invest, you need to maintain the portfolio and that might mean a rejig now and then. You will need to redeem some investments as goals are reached. Your annual capital gains statement must be included in your tax return and taxes must be calculated and paid on your short- and long-term capital gains. Dividend income, if any, also must be accounted for in your tax return. This is an ongoing and never-ending process and will probably outlive you as your corpus is inherited by your nominees.

When you set out on the DIY road, understand that you are taking on yourself all the activities, from deciding your asset allocation, portfolio creation, scheme selection and all the subsequent work of setting up the SIPs and managing the paperwork. In no way am I deterring you from this very satisfying route. But do not underestimate the time this might take. Also, for portfolios beyond a certain size, I have noticed that DIY investors begin to look for some professional help to manage their financial lives.

It is good to begin on your own as you get a good handle of the basics, so if subsequently, you work with a planner, you are much more on top of things. As a DIY investor, you will buy the direct plan, of course. To onboard funds, you need a platform that offers schemes of all the fund houses and allows you to set up features like SIP, STP and SWP. MF Utility is one such platform that has been set up by all the mutual funds contributing to its capital. There is no transaction charge (as of writing this in April 2023—these things can change) and though the site is not as sophisticated as some of the new app-based platforms, there is the comfort of transacting through a pipe that is unlikely to disappear overnight as some apps might.

There are VC-funded fintech firms that are offering to do the KYC for free and have no transaction charge on very smart apps. They too offer the direct plan, but be careful of the readymade portfolios they offer. I found credit risk funds in one such platform's debt bundle. It is very important to see the underlying funds if you are investing through these readymade portfolios.

Then there are execution-only firms that stock brokers offer and these work on the mutual fund platforms of BSE and NSE. You get the direct plan and ease of transaction, but how long these will be free is not clear. There are other entities that also offer a platform, but might have restricted service offerings. For example, they might not have onboarded all the fund houses. They might not have all the onboarding and off-boarding options such as SIP, STP and SWP facilities.

I would look for a long-term stable entity that offers all fund houses and all possible options of entry and exit for my money. Ideally, I would like to do this at zero cost.

If you are still wondering why I have not recommended that you go to each AMC to buy direct online, you have not understood the chapter on portfolios! You need a portfolio approach to your funds and not an individual product route. It is only if you plan to buy just one index fund and one debt fund that a single AMC direct route will work for you.

The distributor route

A distributor of bread is usually a retail shop. Your neighbourhood shopkeeper will vend it and take the embedded commission in the market price that the manufacturer of bread pays him. The shopkeeper will usually have several brands of bread and you either know what you like or might try one or the other to see what you like. There is very little cost to a wrong decision in buying bread as it is a low-value, often-repeated purchase and if you don't like one brand you simply buy something else the next day.

Financial products can never be compared to physical products in this manner. They are invisible, the product is created in your mind at the point of sale and there is information asymmetry, which that means that the manufacturer of a financial product and its seller know far more than you do about the costs and benefits of the product. Therefore, the distributor of a mutual fund is supposed to have far more responsibility than a simple vendor of bread. Or, for that matter, the dealer of a car. Or the seller of a mobile phone connection or broadband. The seller of a mutual fund needs to ensure that the sale is suitable. What this means is that the fund category and the specific scheme being sold work with the age, stage, goals and risk capacity of the investor.

I remember when I was doing a show with NDTV many years ago, the cameraman once came up after the show to ask if he had invested in the right funds. To my horror, I saw that the bank manager had put a low-risk person with goals that were very near into a high-risk sector fund. This was an unsuitable sale. In another industry, selling a life insurance cover to a seventy-five-year-old person with no dependents is unsuitable, to say the least.

SEBI requires mutual fund distributors, or MFDs as they are called, to adhere to a best-practices code and make suitable sales after finding out the requirements of the investor. The MFDs are registered with AMFI and must pass a test before they get a license to sell.

There are more than 1,500 active MFDs in India, with many of them having large cross-country presence. There are mainly two kinds of distributors—corporate and individual.[1] They sell you regular plans and you pay an ongoing trail commission that is embedded in the expense ratio to the distributor. Some distributors offer fairly sophisticated services for portfolio creation, maintenance and managing the tax paperwork. Some distributors such as many banks do quite poorly on the metric of suitable sales and after-sales service.

The registered investment advisor route

Registered investment advisor (RIA) is an entity that is supposed to take a much wider look than a distributor. An RIA should help you construct, maintain and perpetuate your portfolio taking into account your overall net worth, including assets other than mutual funds. Their role is advisory and they charge you a fee. There are limits to the fees put in by the regulator and since these things change off and on and it is better to check the latest rule in place when you read this book.

Investors actually don't want just advice; they also want execution of the suggested portfolio. So RIAs can now help execute your portfolio through a direct plan route. You pay an annual fee and you onboard the direct plan, saving an increasing annual cost on trail commission that a regular plan costs.

The RIAs are a small community today in India. The value proposition of paying for this service is not that well understood. It is only once people understand that just as lawyers and doctors take a fee, so too do financial planners and advisors. On a growing portfolio, you are better off paying a flat fee to an advisor than paying a trail commission forever.

Which route should you take?

Over the years I have had to refuse to help the extended family and friends who would ask for tips and portfolio advice. I am not licensed to commercially practice as of today and I actually prefer to stay in the space of education and financial literacy than manage individual portfolios. But how do you say no to a close family friend or an uncle who is persistent? So, I would ask them to work with a distributor or RIA depending on their preference. The story plays out many times like this: they get their portfolio constructed by the professional but then disappear to try and execute it themselves. They think that this is a one-time event! They get a bunch of funds and start buying direct. But two years down the line, they are in a mess because things change when you do active funds.

My nephew is investing in some funds he has researched that he validates from me. A year down, we find we have to change two schemes. In a portfolio of five, that is a very large amount of churn. One, we had to change since the fund house was sold to an MNC fund house that has not seen great performance of its schemes. The other suffered due to the change in the categories that happened a few years before. If my nephew did not check back with me, he would still be in the old funds. Therefore, do not make the mistake of taking portfolio advice from a distributor as a one-time event. It is a lifelong relationship. Don't mess with it taking a shortcut route to saving his commission.

When you invest in a portfolio of active funds, you need an annual review of schemes. It is just not good enough to take the prescription and buy the medicine yourself. Not only is it a very cheap thing to do, but it classifies you as a non-serious short-term investor. If I was running a commercial advisory, I would certainly refuse to work with a person like that!

So, what should you do? Many investors begin by going DIY, find it is too difficult as the portfolio size increases and then move to either a distributor or an advisor. The advisor supply today is very small, so you may have no option but to work with a distributor. How do you choose one? How do you choose a dentist or a lawyer? You ask your friends and family, you look for recommendations. Do the same for a finance professional.

The distributor or advisor needs to be in harmony with you and your lifestyle choices. There was a distributor who came from a very conservative background and would frown on personal choices such an expensive vacation and luxury items even if the family could afford it. You are better off with somebody who respects your choices around money and yet nudges you in the right direction for your long-term good.

As we come to almost the end of the process, you need to remember one thing: the best ideas mean nothing if they are not actioned. Taking action initially in the financial markets is not an easy task. Begin with small transactions and build up confidence. Beware of inaction and overconfidence—both are enemies of wealth creation.

The pipelines that connect your money to the investments are very important. Unless you have a system in place that makes investing, maintaining and redeeming painless, you will not take action when needed.

You are doing okay if you understand that

1. you need to be good at online banking and have linked your banks to PAN and Aadhaar;
2. you have your KYC in place;
3. you have chosen a platform for executing your investments;
4. your Invest-It account is linked to the platform;
5. you have taken the decision to either go DIY, or through a distributor or RIA; and
6. there are no shortcuts to investing and taking somebody's investing list will not work for you.

14

FUNDS IN MY MONEY BOX

'A place for everything and everything in its place' works not just for everyday life but also for your money box.

In this chapter I will put products in each of the cells of the money box. Not specific names of funds, but categories and options. The hard part of final product choice is left to you to work through yourself or with a planner. I find it just wrong to vend product names without understanding the full extent of the money situation of a person. Even if you work with a planner or distributor, you will know what questions to ask and know whether you can trust the person or not.

Just to refresh your memory from *Let's Talk Money*, we have a money box in which we keep all our financial products. The box has several cells. Each cell is for a defined financial solution starting from cash flows and ending with a cell for intergenerational wealth transfer. You can draw this out on a paper or use an Excel sheet to create it. This can translate into a physical space to keep your papers that establish claim to the investments. Think of a hybrid model with some papers physically kept and others in a digital form. Create folders, clearly label them with the name of the cell. Each folder will have subfolders with names of the financial year and any other relevant document you need to store.

Cell one: cash flows

To get a better handle on where your money goes each month, it is a good idea to separate the spending from the saving. I use a three-account system. All flows of earnings—salary, rent, interest, dividend, profits, bonus, loan repayments—go into one bank account. Label it Income Account. Each month, I withdraw from it and move my monthly spends to a second bank account that I call my Spend-It account. The third account is my Invest-It account where I park my savings. For people who are just beginning on the journey, you can go ahead and use bank accounts. For those who have now learnt to segregate their savings and spending and want to use mutual funds for investments, instead of a third bank account, you can park your savings in a liquid fund. Use a liquid fund that says 'low risk' on the Risk-o-Meter, and this risk metric does not change over the year.

Refresh this in your memory from page 159 in Chapter 7. You need to choose the growth option. It is best to go direct and get an even lower expense ratio than a regular plan.

Table 14.1

Invest-It cell	
Liquid fund	
Growth	✓
Direct	✓
Low on Risk-o-Meter	✓
Low expense ratio	✓

Cell two: emergency funds

This is a stash of cash for when times go wrong. This is the first investment you make. The purpose of an emergency fund is that it is easily available to you when you want it. This means the product you choose must be 'liquid' or easy to sell with a zero or tiny cost of selling. You need between six months to two years in your emergency fund. Six months for those with no dependents and up to two years for those with more dependents and in their fifties. You can use a bank fixed deposit for this cell for safety. Choose a large commercial bank rather than a small bank or a cooperative bank. You can also choose debt funds for this money. You can have a mix of money market and banking and PSU funds in this cell. The money market fund should be low risk on the Risk-o-Meter, and the banking and PSU should be low-to-moderate risk. Choose the growth option and go direct. You can choose a combination of both FD and mutual funds. Keep three months of monthly costs in an FD and the rest in debt funds. For those targeting up to two years of living costs, put six months of living money in an FD and the rest in debt funds to balance between safety and return. We are not looking for high returns from this cell. We are looking for stability, certainty and liquidity.

Table 14.2

Emergency funds cell		
	Money market fund	Banking and PSU fund
Growth	✓	✓
Direct	✓	✓
Low on Risk-o-Meter	✓	
Low to moderate on Risk-o-Meter	✓	✓
Low expense ratio	✓	✓

Cell three: medical insurance

Choose a family floater with at least a Rs 10 lakh sum insured if you live in a large metro. Do look at the medical insurance chapter in *Let's Talk Money* for more on insurance. For those who cannot get a cover—due to a preexisting disease or age—you will need to create a corpus for your medical needs. Use a conservative hybrid fund with a growth option and create a fund of at least Rs 15 to 25 lakh in it depending on your situation. If you need the money for a medical emergency, you can dip into this, if not, well, this is money you can bequeath finally to your kids. But do try and get yourself included in your kids' group insurance plans if possible, even if for a self-payment.

Table 14.3

Medical emergency cell	
Conservative hybrid	
Growth	✓
Direct	✓
Moderate or moderately high on the Risk-o-Meter	✓
Low expense ratio	✓

Cell four: life insurance

The only product you buy is called a term insurance cover. Buy online and buy from a company that has a claim's experience of more than 95 per cent. Do read the life insurance chapter in *Let's Talk Money*. If for whatever reason you are denied a life cover, then you have no option but to aggressively target your retirement corpus. Retirement need not be at sixty. It is the day you are free from going to work to pay your bills. If you cannot buy life cover, then you need to build this go-free money for your dependents as fast as you can. See the retirement cell for options of funds for this purpose.

Cell five: short-term, Almost There goals

Almost There goals are three years or less away from today. Typically, these will be a down payment for a home, money to study further, marriage spend, car or bike down payment, a foreign holiday. The basic rule of thumb is this: the closer the goal to today, the less risk it should be taking. It should also be liquid and easy to get out of at very minimal cost. You need a mix of debt funds in this cell depending on how far and how large your goals are.

For all of these, choose the growth option. Take the direct plan. Liquid funds for needs within three months, money-market funds for needs within two years and for needs between two and three years, use banking and PSU funds.

Table 14.4

Almost There cell			
	Liquid fund	Money market fund	Banking and PSU fund
Growth	✓	✓	✓
Direct	✓	✓	✓
Low on Risk-o-Meter	✓	✓	
Low to Moderate on Risk-o-Meter		✓	✓
Low expense ratio	✓	✓	✓

Cell six: medium-term, In Some Time goals

These are goals that are between three to seven years in the future. These could include buying a house, own higher education and marriage, or kids' higher education and marriage. It becomes already a little difficult to assign exact values to goals that are in the future, but according to our income, we know what we can aspire for. Somebody earning less than Rs 25 lakh a year may not think of buying a farmhouse in Mehrauli that costs double-digit crores in five years, but would manage expectations for a two BHK in a Delhi suburb. To get reality and dreams to meet is the most difficult part when we think about goals that are further away than three years, but it is a good idea to put down a number against a goal and then work back to see how much you need to invest. How much you will need to save will depend on what products you choose to invest in.

The closer your money need is to today, the more allocation into low-to-moderate risk in the categories, and the further away towards seven years the need is, the risk level can rise to moderately high.

Table 14.5

In Some Time cell		
	Banking and PSU fund	Conservative hybrid
Growth	✓	✓
Direct	✓	✓
Low to moderate on Risk-o-Meter	✓	
Moderate on Risk-o-Meter	✓	
Moderately high on Risk-o-Meter		✓
Low expense ratio	✓	✓

Cell seven: long-term, Far Away goals

When you need the money in seven years or more, you can think of taking a much higher risk. Business cycles work their way out over time and short-term end-of-the-world stories also end. Every year for the past fifteen years I've got panicked messages, calls, WhatsApp messages from people who know me asking about whether they should exit their equity investments. It was 2008 crisis, Brexit, Grexit, the US election, the Indian election, China, oil prices are too high, oil has turned negative, pandemic—there is always a new fear factor that tends to spook investors out of the market. I remember, as the market crashed in March 2020 as India got into a tight lockdown to attempt to flatten the curve, one friend exited the market selling his entire portfolio of equity funds. It was a decision based on some fear-mongering PowerPoints sent out by a global investment bank and some stock traders abroad that the market would go on crashing and get out or lose everything. It is when sensible people get caught in the panic zone that I feel the worst regret. The market recovered and was soon back to feeling happy.

History tells us that markets go up and down and your equity investments need the kind of time commitment you show real estate or gold. If you feel afraid at moments of market crash, it is useful to think that we will not go back to living in caves and trundling wheelbarrows around. People will continue to eat, drink, wear clothes and shoes, buy medicine and healthcare, phones, laptops, roads and infra will continue to be built. You are doubting the persistence of human spirit when you think of doomsday scenarios. If you have taken the decision to give your long-term money equity exposure, then leave doubt behind and focus on choosing categories and schemes that work with your needs and risk profile.

The categories shortlisted need to be fitted into the portfolios created in Chapter 12. Just remember the rule: the lower risk portfolio has more of index funds and the higher risk portfolio will have an allocation to small- and mid-cap funds. The very high-risk appetite and capacity investors should only invest in foreign funds.

Table 14.6

Far Away cell				
	Consistent returns	Lower risk in category	Lower expense ratio in category	Low tracking error
Sensex or Nifty 50 index fund			✓	✓
Large- and mid-cap fund	✓	✓	✓	
Mid-cap fund	✓	✓	✓	
Small-cap fund	✓	✓	✓	
Multi-cap fund	✓	✓	✓	
ELSS	✓	✓	✓	
Foreign	✓	✓	✓	

Cell eight: retirement

This is the toughest nut to crack. How much to save for my retirement remains one of the most difficult questions to answer. You need a degree in futurology, math, finance and a crystal ball to figure out how long you will live, what inflation rates will be, what it will cost to live twenty-thirty-forty years from today. People in their seventies today had no idea that they would be spending money on gadgets like smartphones, tablets, laptops and that a part of their monthly bills will be phone bills and data costs. Who would have thought twenty years ago that a five-day stint in a hospital in a large Indian metro will need Rs 5–7 lakh?

The retirement question is this: will I die so soon that my retirement savings will be so much in excess that I would have compromised my lifestyle today for a tomorrow that did not fully play out? Or, will I have more life than money left? Will I have to skimp on lifestyle that I am used to in my old age as I find myself living on and on? The risk for most people in their thirties and forties today is not of dying too soon, but living too long in terms of their money. The retirement ages of fifty-eight and sixty were set when the average age at which people died was in their fifties. The new average is in the seventies and many people live on to their nineties. You are looking at a full twenty-five to thirty years post retirement. That is a lot of years to plan for in the thirty to thirty-five years of your working life.

A small piece of advice: plan to never stop working. You can quit a job, but never quit work. It gives you something to do and it generates fresh income. Some of us dream about perfect retirements in the hills or by the sea, far away from the humdrum of daily lives, far away from all problems. Retirement is actually the time you want your family, community and friends around you. Building a cottage in a place unfamiliar to you is a really bad idea for your old age.

Plan to stay useful all your life. This life is not about whiling away time, but about living fully till the end.

But I am still not getting to the point! Well, here it is—you need between eighteen to thirty-five times your annual spends at age sixty as a retirement corpus. Eighteen times, if you plan to eat out of the corpus so that it finishes by age 100. Thirty-five times, if you plan to leave it all for the kids. A middle-road ratio is twenty-six times. So, if you are spending Rs 20 lakh a year at sixty, plan to have Rs 5.2 crore as a corpus. Another way to think this through is to mark yourself as your grow. By age forty, have three times your annual income for retirement. At age fifty, make that six times. By sixty, you need to have eight times your annual income for your retirement. See the difference in numbers of the two approaches as the difference between incomes and spending. Fifties is the highest earning years with the lowest spending ratios.

Now the even tougher question: in what do you invest to reach your target? The core of your portfolio is the risk-free products like your EPF and PPF. If you are not a part of the organized sector, then you will need to build your own low-risk core of the retirement portfolio. You can include PPF into the safer part of your long-term retirement corpus as well. If some market innovation gets a DIY investor to figure out the expected return on a target maturity fund, then these become great products for long-term accumulation through a passive debt fund.

The equity part of your portfolio needs to have a mix of index, large- and mid-cap, multi-cap, mid- and small-cap funds. The closer you are to retirement, the lower is the mix of small- and mid-caps and the further away you are from retirement, the more risk you can take within your equity allocation.

Table 14.7

Retirement cell				
	Consistent returns	Lower risk in category	Lower expense ratio in category	Low tracking error
PF PPF	Government-guaranteed tax-free products			
Sensex or Nifty 50 index fund			✓	✓
Large- and mid-cap fund	✓	✓	✓	
Mid-cap fund	✓	✓	✓	
Small-cap fund	✓	✓	✓	
Multi-cap fund	✓	✓	✓	
Foreign	✓	✓	✓	

Cell nine: gold

Gold should be no more than 10 per cent of your portfolio as it provides a hedge against inflation. Gold also is a safety asset when there is global distress—as we saw during the 2020 pandemic. You can buy government gold bonds or invest through gold ETFs or index funds. Gold index funds buy gold ETFs of the same fund house and are a way to give better access and liquidity to investors. Gold funds are more liquid than sovereign gold bonds but have costs that the bonds don't have. Depending on your need, choose one or both of these products. Gold bonds can be bought every year to ladder the return since there is a lock-in. A part of the gold allocation can be in a gold fund.

Table 14.8

Gold cell	
	Gold index funds
Growth	✓
Direct	✓
Low expense ratio	✓

Cell ten: real estate

Real estate as an investment has been overrated in India. We forget to count the costs and the number of years of holding that finally give the returns we see. A better way to invest in real estate is through mutual funds called Real Estate Investment Trusts (REITs), but these are yet to find a place in our portfolios as the market is still nascent. One of the reasons that we don't have a formal financial market for real estate assets is the opacity and the presence of black money in the asset. Keep one roof over your head and let go of the temptation of the next Gurgaon. Financial assets are more liquid, cheaper to transact and are better vehicle for tax-paid money.

Cell eleven: estate planning

This is the cell that you create so that the assets you leave your family, if you either have an untimely death or die of old age, are clearly marked out. The paperwork is complete and there is no dispute that you leave behind. Spend lots of time to get this cell right. Your nominations in each bank account, each locker, each mutual fund, insurance policy is done. Your will is done and dusted and your beneficiaries know the location of the papers.

As we go through the various cells, we see the need of several financial products over our life journey to meet many different needs. Mutual funds as a category of investment options has products that meet most of these needs—other than medical and life insurance. But the selection of the categories and the schemes is really important for them to work for you.

We've done a lot of work over the past chapters to get to know this product better. I do hope you have understood that this is not a jadu ki chhari, a magic wand to double and triple money overnight. Be conservative when you begin to invest through funds, build your confidence and then step out into the deep. This has also been my personal journey as I have used the product, made mistakes and then course-corrected. My own portfolio is not the best out there, I'm sure—but it is customized to my life and needs. Do the same for your own investing journey. I wish you a rich money journey.

There are lots of competing products that want to find a place in our money box. Gold, insurance policies, real estate, mutual funds, bonds. It can get confusing, to say the least. Mutual funds have products that solve most money problems other than insurance and a roof over your head.

You are doing okay if you understand that

1. your money box has various cells that need to be filled by different products;
2. each cell will have no more than two schemes for each purpose;
3. each product must compete with the others for a place in your money box;
4. the products must be re-evaluated each year to see if they still qualify;
5. a bad year for an otherwise well-performing consistent scheme is not reason enough to discard it; and
6. too much churn in your money box is a sign that something is not right and needs a fix.

Appendix I

JARGON-FREE INVESTING

Simplicity is underrated. To keep it simple needs discipline, knowledge and patience.

Alpha	Alpha is the outperformance over the benchmark displayed by a fund. I like alpha in funds, other than in index funds.
AMC	Asset Management Company is also known as the mutual fund company. It is the corporate entity that takes care of the business of running the mutual fund and managing investor money.
Asset class	In a thali meal, there are different categories of nutrients. Rice, roti, daal, meat, vegetables, salad, curd, pickle—each comes with its attributes to give a complete meal. Equity, debt, cash, real assets are like

	that. Each has different attributes that give your portfolio a different flavour. Equity for growth, debt for stability and liquidity, gold for inflation hedge and real estate for a roof over your head. You need all of them all the time—just the proportions will differ.
AUM	Assets under management is the term used to indicate how much of investor money the mutual fund is managing on a given day. AUM is measured for each scheme and across all schemes in a fund house and across all fund houses together for the mutual fund industry.
Average maturity	It is the weighted average of the maturity of all the bonds in the portfolio. If there are three bonds with maturity of three, five and ten years, then the average maturity is the average of the three, or six years. This is true if the bonds have equal value in the portfolio, but if a bond has a higher share, then its maturity will influence the average maturity number.
Benchmarks	A standard unit of measurement. By itself data can give few insights, but when compared to the standard observed, we get to know if the performance is higher

	or lower than the average. The average height will differ across countries and therefore each country's tall-ness will be defined by that country's average height.
Beta	Measures volatility or the up and down movements around the average. A fund with a beta of 1 exactly matches the benchmark. A beta more than 1 means that the fund rises and falls more than the market average, a beta less than 1 means that the fund rises and falls less than the market average.
Broad market index	An index that is made up of large, mature companies that have enough shares in the market to provide liquidity. Some of the companies in such an index will be called the 'blue chips' or market leaders that have given steady returns for many years.
Credit risk	The risk that the borrower will not pay interest and principal in time, or at all. This risk is zero for a solvent government like India. This risk is very high in sectors such as real estate. This is a risk to watch out for in a debt mutual fund.
Churn	The practice of brokers and agents moving investors in and out of stocks, insurance policies and other financial products that carry a sales commission with the aim of

harvesting the commission. I don't like investors being churned.

Debt The asset class that includes fixed-return products like fixed deposits, company deposits, PF, PPF, bonds and debt mutual funds. Debt provides stability and liquidity to investors' portfolios.

Demat When the share, bond, mutual fund and insurance certificates are stored electronically and investors get a statement that shows their holdings rather than a physical certificate. Much safer, lower cost and more efficient than trundling physical certificates around.

Direct Direct mode of investing allows investors to buy and sell financial products directly from the manufacturers of the products. Mutual funds have a direct option, so do government bonds through the RBI Direct portal.

Diversification Spreading investments across asset classes that have specific attributes so that the investor is not overinvested in one type of asset. This is a strategy to bring the risk of the portfolio down. A thali meal is an example of a diversified diet.

Dividend	The share from profits that is distributed by the company. This is the profit that remains after all costs and taxes have been paid and the company chooses to distribute rather than reinvest or hold cash.
Duration	The number that links changes in interest rates to changes in bond prices. A duration of 2, for example, means that when interest rates change by 1 per cent, bond prices change (in the opposite direction) by 2 percentage points. The higher the duration, the greater is the interest rate risk. Watch out for this one. It brought the SVB bank down.
Equity	Shares in a business. It is an asset class that is used to build growth in a portfolio. If you don't have your own business, you can participate by buying equity in somebody else's business.
Expense ratio	The percentage of the assets under management of a mutual fund that goes towards costs and profits of the asset management company. The regulator puts ceilings on what funds can charge.
Fund manager risk	The risk of the person or company managing your money taking wrong calls about the products they buy and sell.

Futures	This is an agreement between two parties to buy or sell an underlying asset (such as commodities, currencies or stock indices) at a specific price and date in the future. Futures contracts are standardized, meaning that the size and terms of the contract are predetermined. Mainly used by traders to hedge against volatility or for speculation.
G-secs	Government of India bonds sold by the RBI to raise funds for different tenors—from very short, to very long dates bonds. These are considered safe from credit risk, but not interest rate risk.
Index	It is a selected basket of stocks, bonds, commodities and services from the whole universe of such items, whose prices are averaged out to result in a number. The change in this number, up or down, signals a change in the average price of that group of items.
Indexation	A part of the rise in the price of an asset is inflation. Tax laws allow the investor to inflate the purchasing price of an asset to remove this impact and thereby reduce the profit, and therefore the tax paid on the profit.

Inflation	The rate at which prices rise over the years. It is measured by an index called the cost of living index or the consumer price index.
Load	The embedded commission in the sale price of a financial product. The extent of the investment into the destination asset is reduced by the amount of load or commission paid out to the agent or broker. I don't like loads.
Lock-in	The embargo period in which an asset cannot be sold. This can vary from a few days to a milestone such as retirement age. ELSS funds have a three-year lock-in. Most equity funds might have a one-year lock-in.
Macaulay duration	Another measure of duration. This measures the average time period before which the investor will receive the bond's cash flows. It takes into account the periodic interest blasts from the bond along with the return of principal.
Money market	The market for very short-term fixed income securities such as overnight bonds, commercial paper and very short-term treasuries.

NAV	Net asset value is the price of a unit of a mutual fund. It is the total assets under management divided by the number of units, net of costs. The difference in this over time is used to calculate your return.
Options	It is a contract that gives the holder the right to buy or sell an underlying asset at a specific price, called strike price, and date in the future. It is not an obligation to buy—holder has an option to buy or not.
Portfolio	Think of it like a thali meal—different proportions of nutrients to solve your physical health problems. Different asset classes, and within each asset class, different financial products to solve your financial health issues.
Quartile	When you divide data into four equal parts, sorting from highest to lowest according to some measure of value. A top quartile fund is one that always remains in the top 25 per cent of all funds in terms of returns.
R&T agents	Third-party entities that keep a record of all investor-related details. They take care of updating information like bank changes, contact details, address change. They also keep a record of all transactions made by an investor. Works like a back-office of the mutual fund industry.

Real return	The return after taking into account the impact of inflation. Remove inflation from nominal return to get the real return.
Regular	The regular option in mutual funds is the option of buying a scheme from an agent or broker who gets a trail commission from the AMC. This commission is part of the expense ratio of the fund, making it more expensive than the direct option.
Sensex	The 30 stock Bombay Stock Exchange bellwether index that tracks the top companies of India. The oldest broad market index of the country.
SIP	Systematic investment plan is a route to investing in a mutual fund scheme. It is the regular outflow from an investor's account into a pre-decided scheme for a pre-decided amount.
Sponsor	The entity that sets up the mutual fund business. Usually a financial institution like a bank or public financial institution, a sponsor has some net worth and eligibility criterion before they are allowed to set up a mutual fund in India.
Spot market	A market where the delivery of the security is immediate and not in the future. Cash is exchanged for the security that is delivered immediately.

Standard deviation	The dispersion of all the observed data around the mean. If data points are far away from the mean, then the standard deviation is higher than if they were closer to the mean. A high standard deviation in a mutual fund indicates higher risk.
STP	Systematic transfer plan is the option that allows investors to create a holding fund that is dipped into periodically to infuse the destination fund with money. Typically used to stagger a large lump sum of money over six months to a year to average out the stock market volatility.
SWP	Systematic withdrawal plan allows investors to redeem either a fixed number of units or money at periodic intervals by setting up a mandate to redeem the units held in a particular scheme of a mutual fund.
Tracking error	The difference in the performance of an index fund from the index it is tracking. Ideally there should be no difference in the performance of an index fund and the index.

Trust	The entity that holds the funds of investors in India. Trusts have very strict rules and this has prevented sponsors or AMCs from running away with investor money.
Yield	A measure of return over a period of time. It is indicated in a percentage number based on the current value of the product.

Appendix 2

STORIES TO HELP YOU FIX YOUR PORTFOLIO

Everyone has a unique story. One size never fits all.

The new gig worker

Suraj Gupta is a video editor. He is twenty-eight and his life changed with the burst of video blogging and reels on social media. From a stressful, acrimonious media job where he was working twelve hours a day for Rs 45,000 a month, he began doing gig jobs over the pandemic and then in January 2022, set out on his own. His business took off and he found himself hiring two other people to help him keep track of the work that just flowed in. He is doing a huge multiple of what he was getting as a salary, but his income is erratic and he finds it difficult to save not knowing when the flow of money will stop. How should he plan his finances?

Suraj needs to separate out his business expenses from his personal ones. He should use my three-account system and modify it to add a fourth account—the Business

Expense account. Use one bank account to gather all the inflows into his life. Then take the money he will spend on personal needs into a second bank account. The amount allocated for business needs goes into a third account and savings into a fourth account—the Invest-It account. He should use a liquid fund to target three months of expenditure for both personal and business needs as a safety net for irregular business income flows. He must create an emergency fund that looks after two years of his spends. Once this is done, he must now begin investing for the future. In the month when there is a slowdown in income (sometimes clients take time to pay), he can get money overnight from his liquid fund that is connected to his spending accounts. Discipline and systems are going to be of great use to Suraj as he grows. A financial mess can torpedo a fledgling business. He should hire a good tax planner to help with his GST and other tax needs.

The rich old uncle

Raman JV is seventy-five years old. Single with no dependents, he is a retired college professor who lives with his brothers (also not married) in their ancestral home in Old Delhi. Raman has a pension that is more than enough for his needs and he has assets worth over Rs 5 crore in some properties, bank deposits and insurance policies. He wants to consolidate his assets and buy only mutual funds as they are easier to bequeath. He wants to leave everything to his sister's daughter in the US who is in her late twenties. What should his investing pattern look like?

The cookie-cutter answer to this question is that looking at his age, Raman should be a conservative investor and stay away from too much equity. But a closer look at his profile tells a different story. He does not need the money from his investments as he is well-funded for life. He needs a cushion for medical emergencies and should put away as much as a crore in a conservative hybrid fund for a lavish allocation for an emergency. The rest of the money he can put to use to grow it so that by the time his niece inherits, she gets a portfolio that is good for her age and stage. He should invest in a mix of index, mid-cap and small-cap funds in a direct growth plan. He should be careful to put his niece's name in the nomination of the investments, make a will and give her contact details in that. He should inform his niece of his intentions so that she knows that she needs to make a claim.

Going solo

Radhika Patel is a divorced thirty-five year old woman with no kids. She lives alone in her fully owned flat in Surat. She has her own web design business that more than takes care of her needs. She has no dependents, her parents live in Vadodara and have enough pension funds. She wants to begin investing for her old age and wants to put away Rs 25 lakh a year towards her retirement that she thinks will begin by age sixty. She has no interest in managing her money and would prefer to spend her time in increasing her business. She is looking for a financial planner to help her. What should she do?

Half of Radhika's problems are solved because she has decided that she will not do it herself and execute every tip she gets on where to invest. People underestimate the power of such a simple decision: I can't do this myself and will get help, pay for it and spend my time where I want to. She should begin her search for a distributor or planner the way she would find a dentist. Look for recommendations from friends and family first. Ideally, she should choose somebody in the same city she lives in. She can check for a distributor name on the AMFI website.[1] She can check for a fee-only financial advisor on this site.[2]

If she decides to go with a registered financial advisor, she should choose a flat fee option rather than a percentage of her assets under management. She should ensure that she is in a direct plan if she is paying a fee. Radhika should read *Let's Talk Money* and *Let's Talk Mutual Funds* to know what to look for in the funds recommended by the distributor. She should specially read Chapters 9, 10, 11 and 12 of this mutual fund book.

The first job

V Saritha is very excited about her first job. At twenty-five she is getting to start her life with a nice CTC of Rs 20 lakh a year in a bank job. Though she has studied finance, six months into the job she realizes that while she has studied math and finance, she has no idea what to do with her salary. She finds she has no control over her money and has no idea where her money gets spent. Nobody ever taught her personal money management in school, college or business school. She has no particular goals but feels that she needs to do some investing. She wants a mix of safety, growth and money in a few years to go for higher studies if she feels the need to change career directions. How should she begin planning?

Saritha knows the basics of numbers and is an MBA with a focus on finance, so she should set up her own portfolio. She should open an account with a platform that allows her to invest direct. She needs a mix of liquidity and growth. She should set up the three-account system so that she is able to separate her savings from her spending. She should observe her spending flows for six months and get an idea of how much she can save each month. Next, she should begin investing in a money market fund to begin her emergency fund. That should be equal to six months of her spends. Once that is done, she begins to invest for the future. Since there are no defined goals at the moment, it is fair to split her savings into three equal parts and invest them for the short-, medium- and long-term needs. She should revisit Chapter 9 in this book to see what categories she needs to invest in and then Chapters 10, 11 and 12 to create her portfolio and choose her own schemes.

NOTES

4: The Choice Set

1 Monika Halan, 'Reducing choice, not well-being', *Mint*, 3 November 2015, https://www.livemint.com/Money/dTpbbbtSpIrQKGQ8CiqeFP/Reducing-choice-not- wellbeing.html

5: Entry and Exit Options

1 Hugh Hoikwang Kim and Santosh Anagol, 'The impact of shrouded fees: evidence from a natural experiment in the Indian mutual funds market', 3 August 2010, https://papers.ssrn.com/sol3/papers.cfm?abstract_id=1660988

2 The list can be seen on the AMFI website here: https://www.amfiindia.com/investor-corner/online-center/locate-mf-distributor.aspx

6: Costs, Returns and Benchmarks

1 You can read the report that we produced here: 'Financial well-being: report of the committee on investor awareness and protection', Ministry of Finance, https://www.finmin.nic.in/sites/default/files/D%20Swarup%20Committee%20Report.pdf
2 You can read it here: 'Proposal of review of total expense ratio of mutual find schemes', https://www.sebi.gov.in/sebi_data/meetingfiles/oct-2018/1539576106009_1.pdf
3 You can use this link to see the latest NAV for all funds: https://www.amfiindia.com/net-asset-value
4 You can go to the AMFI site to see the names of the firms and the benchmarks allowed for first-tier use by funds: https://www.amfiindia.com/research-information/other-data/listofbenchmarkindices.
5 I find sites like valueresearchonline.com and Morningstar.in good to check for benchmark details of the schemes I am comparing.

7: Risk

1 Peter Dizikes, 'Study: commercial air travel is safer than ever', MIT News, 23 January 2020, https://news.mit.edu/2020/study-commercial-flights-safer-ever-0124
2 This gets complicated very quickly, but those interested can read this SEBI order: https://www.sebi.gov.in/legal/circulars/nov-2018/guidelines-for-enhanced-disclosures-by-credit-rating-agencies-cras-_40988.html
3 You can see it on the AMFI website here: https://www.amfiindia.com/investor-corner/online-center/riskmeterinformation
4 You can read the article here: 'What is a risk-o-meter and how has it changed?', 22 March 2021, https://www.valueresearchonline.com/stories/49145/what-is-a-risk- o-meter-and-how-has-it-changed

8: Taxes

1 You can see it on the Income Tax Department, Government of India website here: https://incometaxindia.gov.in/
2 You can check out all the rates on the Central Board of Indirect Taxes and Customs website here: https://cbic-gst.gov.in/gst-goods-services-rates.html
3 You can refer to this document on the Income Tax Department website to see all the avenues for getting this deduction: https://incometaxindia.gov.in/Pages/tools/deduction-under-section-80c.aspx
4 You can see the rates and the tax benefits you have to give up on the Income Tax Department website here: https://incometaxindia.gov.in/Tutorials/2%20Tax%20Rates.pdf
5 This is a useful resource available on the Income Tax Department website: https://incometaxindia.gov.in/Pages/faqs.aspx
6 You can get the indexation table and formula at this government site: https://incometaxindia.gov.in/tutorials/15-%20ltcg.pdf
7 Again, these rules keep changing and you can keep up using this link on the Income Tax Department website: https://incometaxindia.gov.in/tutorials/16.%20exemption%20under%2054.pdf

9: Reducing Choice

1 AMFI website, New Fund Offers: https://www.amfiindia.com/new-fund-offer
2 Value Research, New Fund Offers: https://www.valueresearchonline.com/funds/new- fund-offers/

10: Choosing Schemes

1 Value Research, Mutual Fund Monitor: https://www.valueresearchonline.com/funds/fund-category/
2 Morning Star: https://www.morningstar.in/featured-reports.aspx

3 CRISIL, Mutual Fund Ranking: https://www.crisil.com/en/home/what-we-do/financial-products/mf-ranking.html
4 Value Research, Fund Compare: https://www.valueresearchonline.com/funds/fund-compare/
5 You can see it on the AMFI website here: https://www.amfiindia.com/investor-corner/online-center/riskmeterinformation

11: Index Investing

1 You can see the list on the NSE website here: https://www.nseindia.com/market-data/live-market-indices
2 AMFI website: https://www.amfiindia.com/research-information/other-data/mf-scheme-performance-details
3 AMFI website: https://www.amfiindia.com/research-information/other-data/tracking_errordata

12: Portfolios

1 AMFI website: https://www.amfiindia.com/investor-corner/knowledge-center/tax-corner.html

13: How to Buy

1 You can see a list on the AMFI site here: https://www.amfiindia.com/locate-your-nearest-mutual-fund-distributor-details

Appendix 2: Stories to Help You Fix Your Portfolio

1 AMFI website: https://www.amfiindia.com/locate-your-nearest-mutual-fund-distributor- details
2 Association of Registered Investment Advisers: https://aria.org.in/directory/members

- All tables are author's own unless specified otherwise.

ACKNOWLEDGEMENTS

Gratitude to The Mother and Sri Aurobindo for their guidance and grace.

For their undying patience and unrelenting prodding, Ananth Padmanabhan and Sachin Sharma of HarperCollins India. This book is two years late. But I will just blame COVID-19 and its accompanying devastation for the delay.

This book might never have been written if I had not taught the postgraduate students at National Institute of Securities Markets (NISM) a course on mutual funds in 2022. The rigour that went into my class notes helped me refine this book. A big shout-out to the 2024 Securities Market batch—thank you for (mostly) not sleeping in my class.

Special thanks to the copy editor of this book, Shreya Lall—thank you for your edits and understanding my slightly hat-ke writing style.

The cover picture shoot was a lot of fun. I have to thank ex-colleague and now independent professional Vivan Mehra for not getting irritated at all the interventions Gautam Chikermane made in trying to get that perfect shot.

To the cover designer, Bonita Shimray, all I can say is that long distance is not a patch on doing the cover prep and execution in person. We missed you. But we still managed to follow your instructions and hopefully delivered a good product.

Thank you Saurav Das for the final cover and being patient with my requests for more colour options.

This book would not have been possible without Kayezad E. Adajania, ex-colleague and friend. His other name is Dr Fund. He knows mutual funds better than they know themselves. He was one message away for resources, explanations and data. Thanks K.

To the SEBI Mutual Fund Advisory Committee that I served from 2009 to 2021 for giving me a voice in getting the rules right for investors. A lot of my insights are based on the work we did together over the twelve years on that committee. I wish investors knew how much effort goes into each piece of regulation that comes out of the committee in the mutual fund space.

To the readers of *Let's Talk Money* who kept reaching out to ask when the promised mutual fund book will be out. I had left a teaser in the earlier book promising this one. And you guys just did not let go—so here is the book. I hope that it is worth your time.

To all my readers, listeners and viewers, heartfelt gratitude for making my work meaningful. Every message from you that tells me that you've benefited from my books, talks and videos makes my day. This is more than money for me.

To my neuroscientist daughter Meera whom I track shamelessly on social media if she forgets to message every day.

To Gautam, my husband, the pressure for a 'more better' story has now become one for a 'more better' book. And for turning every dinner table conversation into a panel discussion. *Sahi hai*!

INDEX

ABOUT THE AUTHOR

Monika Halan's career spans across media, public policy and financial education. She is the founder of Dhan Chakra Financial Education and author of the bestselling book *Let's Talk Money* (HarperCollins, 2018). She has public policy experience and has served on several high-profile Government of India and SEBI committees. She has worked across various media organizations in India, including *Mint*, *The Economic Times* and *The Indian Express*, and was the editor of *Outlook Money*. She has run four successful TV series around personal finance on *NDTV*, *Zee* and *Bloomberg India*.

She is an MA in economics from the Delhi School of Economics and MA in journalism studies from the University of Wales. A Yale World Fellow (2011), Halan is based in New Delhi.

You can reach out to her at mailme@monikahalan.com